Indonesia

Nicola Frost

Oxfam

Oxfam
Community Aid Abroad

樂施會
Oxfam
Hong Kong

n(o)vib
OXFAM NETHERLANDS

First published by Oxfam GB in 2002

Available from:
Bournemouth English Book Centre, PO Box 1496, Parkstone, Dorset, BH12 3YD, UK
tel: +44 (0)1202 712933; fax: +44 (0)1202 712930; email: oxfam@bebc.co.uk

USA: Stylus Publishing LLC, PO Box 605, Herndon, VA 20172-0605, USA
tel: +1 (0)703 661 1581; fax: +1 (0)703 661 1547; email: styluspub@aol.com

For details of local agents and representatives in other countries, consult our website: http://www.oxfam.org.uk/publications or contact Oxfam Publishing, 274 Banbury Road, Oxford OX2 7DZ, UK
tel: +44 (0)1865 311 311; fax: +44 (0)1865 312 600; email: publish@oxfam.org.uk

Our website contains a fully searchable database of all our titles, and facilities for secure on-line ordering.

Oxfam GB is a registered charity, no. 202 918, and is a member of Oxfam International.

Printed by
Information Press, Eynsham

All photographs © Tantyo Bangun 2002 (tbangun@indo.net.id)

Series designed by
Richard Morris, Stonesfield Design
Typeset in Scala and Gill Sans.

Contents

Introduction

▲ *Mount Merapi, an active volcano, overshadows a mosque in Magelang, Central Java.*

Modern Indonesia is a land of extremes: a huge, sprawling archipelago of tropical islands, home to more than 200 million people; a secular state with the world's largest Muslim population; extraordinary economic growth, followed by equally spectacular monetary collapse; political crisis and the threat of national disintegration; widespread ethnic and religious violence; and environmental meltdown. But what lies behind the dramatic headlines? What is it like to live and work in Indonesia today? And what are its people's hopes and fears for the future?

A diverse geography ...

Reflecting the borders of the Dutch colonial empire, Indonesia stretches 5000 kilometres from the tip of Aceh in the west to the border with Papua New Guinea to the east, taking in three time-zones along the way. Estimates vary, but there are around 17,000 islands, up to 6000 of them inhabited. Habitats range from fertile rice paddies to primary rainforests, and from coral atolls to upland savannah and snow-capped mountains. Great arcs of live and dormant volcanoes stretch across the various island chains. As a result, agriculture – whether intensive rice farming on carefully managed terraces, or shifting cultivation in upland forests – is an important activity for Indonesians. Its natural beauty and variety make Indonesia a popular destination for tourists.

Not surprisingly, such an extensive and varied landscape is home to an impressive array of flora and fauna, ranging from the endangered Sumatran tigers and Javanese rhinos to fearsome Komodo dragons and *Rafflesia arnoldi*, the largest flower in the world, found only in parts of Sumatra, whose blooms can grow up to one metre in diameter. Eastern Indonesia is on the 'Australian' side of the Wallace Line, which divides Asian fauna from Australian types; so marsupials are found there,

◀ *A Balinese Hindu priest prays at the feet of a concrete policeman in the middle of a busy road. In Bali, religion is an important part of everyday and community life.*

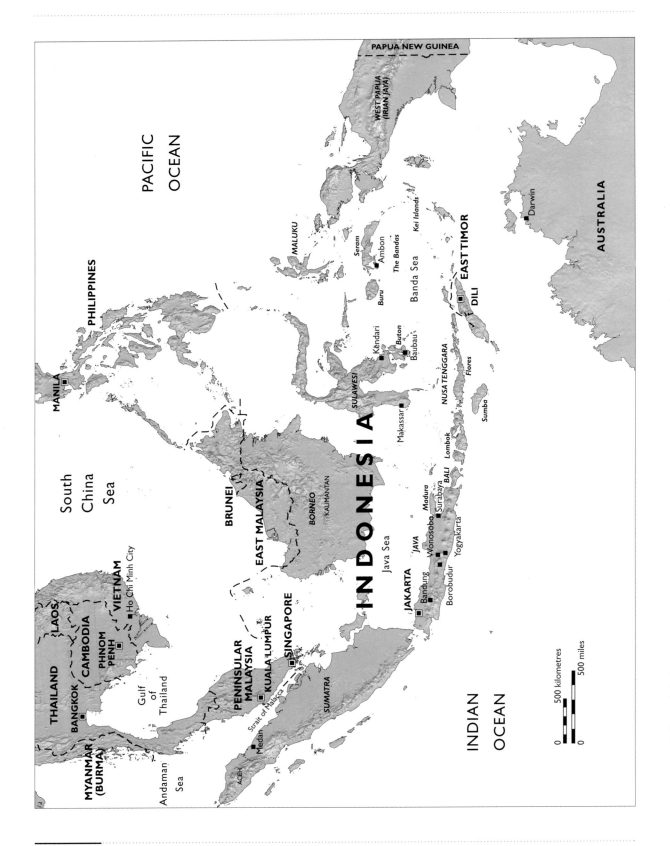

PAPUA NEW GUINEA

WEST PAPUA (IRIAN JAYA)

PACIFIC OCEAN

AUSTRALIA

Darwin

MALUKU

Seram

Ambon

The Bandas

Kei Islands

Banda Sea

Buru

EAST TIMOR

DILI

PHILIPPINES

Kendari

Buton

Baubau

NUSA TENGGARA

SULAWESI

Flores

MANILA

Makassar

Sumba

South China Sea

BRUNEI

EAST MALAYSIA

BORNEO

KALIMANTAN

INDONESIA

Java Sea

BALI

Lombok

Madura

Surabaya

JAVA

Wonosobo

Yogyakarta

JAKARTA

Bandung

Borobudur

THAILAND

LAOS

VIETNAM

BANGKOK

CAMBODIA

PHNOM PENH

Ho Chi Minh City

PENINSULAR MALAYSIA

KUALA LUMPUR

SINGAPORE

Gulf of Thailand

Strait of Malacca

SUMATRA

Medan

ACEH

MYANMAR (BURMA)

Andaman Sea

INDIAN OCEAN

500 kilometres

500 miles

0

0

▲ A lush tropical landscape on the island of Buton, South-East Sulawesi

◀ Map of Indonesia showing places featured in this book

▼ Buton: typical home of Bajau people, or 'sea gypsies', built on stilts about 200 metres from the shore

along with the dramatic birds of paradise. Farther west, orang utans (the name means 'man of the forest') inhabit the extensive rainforests.

More than 80 per cent of Indonesian territory is sea. This is without doubt a maritime nation, oriented towards the sea as a means of communication and a vital natural resource. Indonesia is home to many famous sailing peoples; the ports of Makassar and Surabaya are some of the busiest in South-East Asia, important focal points for national and international trade. Many other Indonesians base their lives and livelihoods along the shoreline. Indonesians are, perhaps as a result, great travellers; wherever you go, it is common to meet people from all over the archipelago. Some of this population movement is spontaneous; some is sponsored by the government, which until 2000 operated a transmigration policy to encourage movement to the 'outer islands', in an attempt to relieve the pressure on the densely populated islands of Java and Bali.

Indonesia is extremely rich in natural resources of all kinds: its forests stretch over more than 225 million acres; there are large deposits of oil and gas, and substantial supplies of many metals and minerals, including tin, copper, nickel, and even gold. Add to this the extensive and abundant fishing grounds, and the fertile volcanic soil of many islands, and it is clear that Indonesia does not lack the raw materials for success. But decades of vigorous government-supported exploitation without proper regard for conservation have depleted many of these resources to critical levels, and endangered the livelihoods of local people who depend on a healthy eco-system.

... and a diverse population

Not only does Indonesia span just about every possible wildlife habitat, but in cultural terms it is difficult to think of a country more diverse. Indonesians are rice farmers, traders, sailors, city slickers, artists, fisherfolk, tour guides, hunter-gatherers, and civil servants. They are Sundanese, Moluccan, Chinese, Papuan, Minang, Bugis, and Balinese.

► *A mosque attendant in Java*

They are Muslims, Christians, Hindus, Buddhists, and animists. They live in longhouses, city apartments, bamboo huts, and historic palaces. It is very difficult to generalise.

Western notions of 'Indonesian' culture are often limited to graceful young Balinese dancers with elaborate eye make-up, and Javanese shadow puppets enacting ancient legends. This is only part of the picture. Contemporary Indonesia enjoys a wide range of cultural influences, both traditional and modern. At ceremonies and concerts, the sound of the *gamelan* – a traditional instrument, composed of a series of bronze gongs – is heard; but if you visit an Indonesian home, or switch on the television, you are just as likely to hear *dangdut* – a kind of popular music with a strong beat, influenced by Hindu and Arabic music – or Western rock music. Similarly, a long-established tradition of producing rich and intricate textiles often combines ancient motifs with more modern designs; *batik* makers and *ikat* weavers are constantly experimenting with new ideas and interpretations.

▼ *An old woman weaving an* ikat *cloth, East Sumba*

Around 85 per cent of Indonesians are Muslim; nine per cent are Christian, and the rest a mixture of Hindus, Buddhists, and followers of indigenous religions. These figures disguise the fact that many Indonesians are nominally adherents of one of the major world religions, yet maintain strong traditional beliefs, often related to animism or ancestor cults. In many communities the two systems co-exist quite happily and have evolved together over many years; it is difficult to determine where one ends and the other begins.

Early history, colonialism, and independence

The sprawling collection of islands that make up modern Indonesia have little shared history that pre-dates the colonial period. Although some empires did have temporary influence over wide stretches of the archipelago, in general the rise and fall of successive Javanese and Sumatran kingdoms made little impact on the Dayaks of upland Borneo, or the Dani in the interior of West Papua. Chinese, Arab, and Indian traders had already been in contact with the archipelago for centuries, but Europeans were first attracted to the East Indies in the sixteenth century by the scent of spice – cloves and nutmeg – wafting from the eastern islands. There followed several centuries of trade, treaties, and wars as a succession of Portuguese, Spanish, Dutch, and English explorers fought for control of this valuable commodity. The Dutch eventually prevailed, and gradually began to establish an empire which came to include all of present-day Indonesia. Life under the Dutch was very difficult for those who were co-opted into working on colonial plantations; for others in more remote areas, the colonial influence was relatively slight.

Taking advantage of the new political climate after the end of the Second World War, Indonesia declared its independence in 1945. The idealism of the nationalist movement quickly gave way to the need to manage a huge and diverse nation. By 1959, President Sukarno's revolutionary administration was replaced by a system of 'guided democracy', or government by decree. In 1965, a mysterious coup attempt put General Suharto in charge, after which began two years of killing and mayhem as suspected supporters of the Communist Party from all over the country were rounded up and killed. Up to half a million people are believed to have died.

President Suharto's New Order regime dominated all aspects of Indonesian life for the next 32 years. Backed by powerful military forces, a heavily centralised and repressive State limited the authority of traditional leaders, controlled the exploitation of natural resources, restricted trade-union activity, censored the media, and generally made it difficult for anyone to disagree with the government. Those charged with subversion risked long periods in prison without trial, and 'disappearances' of dissidents were not uncommon. Corruption was endemic within the bureaucracy, and overt nepotism ensured that many government contracts were exclusively available to companies owned by the Suharto family and their friends.

▲ *Almost one-third of Indonesians live in urban areas. The capital, Jakarta, is a modern, busy metropolis, crowded with skyscrapers and choked with traffic.*

In the 1980s, an aggressive policy of development through industrialisation turned Indonesia into one of the 'Asian tiger' economies. The cities swelled as people moved in from the countryside to work in the new factories. Many observers hoped that increased prosperity would encourage the development of a more liberal society. Yet as Indonesians became wealthier, healthier, and better educated than ever before, the regime became increasingly corrupt and repressive. Finally, in late 1997, the Asian economic meltdown revealed the true extent of financial mismanagement and plunged the country into crisis. The Indonesian currency, the *rupiah*, was devalued by 70 per cent, and millions of people were impoverished. The New Order regime could not withstand the wave of protest that followed, and President Suharto was forced to resign in May 1998. Since then, a succession of leaders have largely failed to determine a clear political direction for Indonesia, as the country struggles with the challenges of democratisation.

Facing the future

Indonesia has undergone some dramatic and sometimes painful changes in recent years. The environmental havoc inflicted by the droughts and floods of the weather system called *El Niño*, combined with poor controls on the exploitation of natural resources, threatens many Indonesian eco-systems. The economic crisis continues to affect the lives of many of its citizens. Political upheaval following the resignation of President Suharto, after more than three decades of repressive rule, has brought democratic elections and increased freedoms for individuals and civil society alike, but it has also led to instability and violence in some areas. Many advances towards a more equal and democratic society have been made, but the future of the reformation process is by no means assured. An entire generation has grown up knowing only the disempowering politics of the New Order. Without the figure of Suharto to rally against, the movement for change has lost direction and momentum.

The past few years have been difficult and challenging ones for Indonesia and its people. But the story is not one of complete despair and social breakdown. Indonesia has largely avoided the chaos repeatedly predicted for it by many commentators, a fact which is a testament to the continued courage, resilience, and creativity of its people. This book aims to show that, despite the complex series of crises which have hit the international headlines, there is much positive activity going on behind the scenes, and initiatives at the local level which are forward-looking and innovative.

▼ *A carpenter at work in a camp for displaced people, Ambon. Indonesians have responded to the nation's political and economic crisis with energy and a determination to rebuild their lives.*

Pre-history to post-colony: Indonesia until 1998

Indonesia has one of the longest continuous records of human habitation in the world. The fossilised remains of 'Java Man' – now known as *Homo erectus erectus* – were discovered in central Java, providing evidence for human occupation dating back well over a million years. Around 15,000 years ago, Mongoloid people from the Asian mainland migrated into Indonesia, pushing the existing Austro-melanesian inhabitants eastwards. People from eastern Indonesia today commonly have darker skin and curlier hair than those from western Indonesia, an indication of their Melanesian origins.

▲ *A man with his pet parrot, West Sumba. His dark skin and curly hair are typical of eastern Indonesians.*

Classical kingdoms

It is difficult to talk about a common Indonesian political history before the later colonial period. Although there were extensive trading networks, the archipelago was a fragmented collection of kingdoms, sultanates, and village-states, often in competition with each other, and frequently at war. Some great empires did emerge, however, exercising control over land beyond their immediate centres of power. The southern Sumatran kingdom of Sriwijaya, for example, controlled the Strait of Malacca, an important trading route, for much of the period between the seventh and the eleventh centuries. The Sjailendra dynasty was responsible for building the great Buddhist temple of Borobudur in central Java, between 770 and 825.

The last – and one of the most successful – Javanese kingdoms was that of Majapahit, which rose to prominence after successfully defeating a Mongolian invasion in 1292. From 1330 to 1364, Majapahit's chief minister was the great Gajah Mada, commemorated now in the name of one of

Indonesia's most prestigious universities, based in Yogyakarta. During this period Majapahit claimed that it could extract tribute from most of what is now Indonesia. In many ways it might be seen as the prototypical Indonesian state, well before the eras of colonial influence or nationalist rhetoric. The power of Majapahit was finally curbed by the increasing influence of Islam in the late fifteenth century.

Europeans and the lure of spice

▲ Hindu temples on the Prambanan plain, Central Java – built in the eighth century, around the same time as the nearby Buddhist temple at Borobudur

The commodity that first lured the Europeans to the Far East, and caused fierce conflicts between Portuguese, Spanish, English, and Dutch seafarers, was spice: specifically, cloves, nutmeg, and mace (the blood-red covering of the nutmeg). These precious plants, which grew only in the remote eastern Islands of Maluku, were literally worth more than their weight in gold. Although western Indonesian kingdoms, along with Arab and Chinese traders, had been doing business with local spice-growers for centuries, the first European contact with the Spice Islands, as they became known, was in the early sixteenth century. In 1511, Portuguese traders established a base at Malacca on the Malay peninsula and began to explore the region, establishing a monopoly on the spice trade. When this arrangement broke down, the Portuguese were expelled, leaving the way open for the Dutch to establish their own agreements with the local sultans.

▼ Wooden ships in Surabaya harbour. Many Indonesian islands were important trading centres for centuries before the arrival of European explorers.

From the beginning of the seventeenth century the newly formed Dutch East India Company initiated an aggressive policy, designed to protect the spice monopoly and consolidate the Dutch position in the Indies. The English did not finally surrender their claims to some islands until 1667. The terms of the deal indicate the importance of the Spice Islands to European trading interests at the time: England agreed to exchange its claim to Run Island in the Banda group for the island of Manhattan, then part of the Dutch settlement of New Amsterdam, in North America.

With the Europeans came Christianity: first Catholicism through the Portuguese, then Protestantism with the Dutch. Portuguese missionaries arrived around the middle of the sixteenth century, and the Dutch Reformed Church first established itself in Ambon, Maluku, at the beginning of the seventeenth century. Many conversions have been much more recent. When Indonesia achieved independence, only ten per cent of people in the region of Toraja, in south Sulawesi, were Christian; now more than 80 per cent are nominal Christians. Eastern Indonesia has the largest Christian population, reflecting the pattern of European settlement in the Indies.

Sharing a religion with the colonisers had its advantages. Ambonese Christians, for example, were educated in Dutch-language schools years before educational opportunities were extended to the wider population, and they enjoyed considerable privileges within colonial society. It is perhaps not surprising, then, that 50,000 Christians from Ambon and the surrounding islands elected to settle in the Netherlands after Independence.

Living with empire

By the eighteenth century, demand for spices in Europe was beginning to decline, but the Dutch were now committed to more than simple trade treaties with the East: they were establishing an empire. It was a slow process; Java came under Dutch control in the eighteenth century, and by the end of the nineteenth century Sumatra had joined it. Many parts of Nusa Tenggara, Sulawesi, Kalimantan, and West Papua, however, remained largely free of Dutch intervention until the early twentieth century, and East Timor remained under Portuguese control until 1974.

The impact of colonial rule differed from place to place. Coastal Islamic trading states were stifled by Dutch-imposed trading restrictions, but sultanates in Kalimantan and Sumatra which were involved in the oil and plantation businesses benefited from the European presence. The Dutch ruled much of the archipelago indirectly through local leaders, leaving local traditions largely undisturbed. Many upland societies were protected from outside influence by their lack of central authority, which gave little leverage for external powers to manipulate. A few areas, such as Aceh, in the far west of Sumatra, fiercely resisted Dutch rule; although the Dutch could be said to have conquered Aceh by 1913, the Aceh War lasted intermittently from 1873 to 1942.

During the nineteenth century, the Dutch came under increasing pressure to extract revenue from their empire. The Cultivation System (*Cultuurstelsel*), devised in the 1830s, transformed Javanese agriculture by establishing large plantations, growing cash crops such as coffee, rubber, and sugar cane, worked by forced labour from three-quarters of a million Javanese households. This tended to accentuate social and economic differences within rural Javanese society, with members of the peasant elite manipulating the system to their advantage. Local leaders, responsible to the Dutch authorities for crop collection, could exploit their position and impose even heavier burdens on the peasants. Ultimately, however, the

Dutch were shaping an independent indigenous aristocracy into a salaried civil service, and tightening their grip on the lives of ordinary peasants. Although the Cultivation System greatly increased export revenue, it was the Dutch, not the Javanese, who grew richer. A reduction in food production led to widespread famine. Even after the system was dismantled in the 1880s, large-scale export production continued through private firms. Peasants were often forced into renting their land to the sugar factories for sugar-cane production, and then working on the plantation in order to pay off debts.

By the early twentieth century, an unlikely nationalist movement had begun to develop, bringing together ordinary people and the elite, communists and Javanese aristocrats, Hindus and Muslims. At the same time, an indigenous intellectual class was gaining influence. A sense of national unity began to develop; perhaps surprisingly, it proved stronger than regional ties. A number of uprisings during the 1920s and 1930s, however, came to nothing, and it seemed that independence was very far off. Then world war broke out, and the Japanese arrived.

Occupation and independence: building a nation

Japanese troops invaded Indonesia in January 1942, and controlled Indonesian territory until Japan's surrender to the Allies in August 1945. The Japanese used the forced labour of tens of thousands of people in mines and for road and railway construction. Food was requisitioned to support the war effort, creating famine in many areas. Details have emerged only recently of the women who were taken into sexual slavery as 'comfort' for Japanese soldiers.

Although the Japanese occupation was oppressive and harsh, it did provide certain opportunities for the nationalist movement. Dutch officials were replaced by Indonesians, who gained practical experience of administration. The nationalist leaders saw the Japanese occupation as a necessary evil – a stepping stone between Dutch rule and full independence. As Japan's fortunes in the war worsened, it prepared to create an Indonesian puppet state. Before this could happen, however, Sukarno declared Indonesia's independence, on 17 August 1945.

The Dutch, aided by Allied troops, initially tried to regain control of the territory. This did not prove either successful militarily or popular politically in the post-war climate. Spirited resistance against the Allied advance, though ultimately unsuccessful, only boosted support for the republic. Eventually, in 1949, the Dutch established a federal state – Republik Indonesia Serikat (RIS). West Papua remained exclusively in Dutch hands. On 17 August 1950 the RIS was dissolved, and the Republic of Indonesia became an independent state at last.

PANCASILA

On 1 June 1945, Sukarno presented his vision for the new Indonesian state. The five points of the doctrine of *Pancasila* are included in the Preamble to the Constitution, and provide the basis for Indonesian nationalist ideology:

- Belief in God
- National Unity
- Humanitarianism
- People's Sovereignty
- Social Justice and Prosperity

While *Pancasila* was originally designed to unite a very diverse society, in the 1980s it was reinterpreted as the 'sole guiding principle' (*azas tunggal*) for all social and political activity. In the authoritarian New Order, instigated by Suharto in 1966, *Pancasila* prohibited adversarial politics based on class, race, or religion, and severely restricted the activities of political parties, trade unions, and religious organisations.

▲ *The mythical* garuda *bird, a national symbol associated with* Pancasila.

Government from 1950 to 1955 involved a series of unstable coalitions as the new nation struggled to get to grips with party politics. Secret power-sharing deals took the place of a clear vision for Indonesia's future. Sukarno regarded the idea of party-based parliamentary democracy as a Western concept unsuitable for Indonesia. In 1957 he unveiled his vision of Guided Democracy, a specifically Indonesian form of politics, whereby consensus emerges through discussion, rather than through voting. In practice it weakened political parties and greatly increased the power of the President. It also confirmed the role of the military as an inextricable element of both government and national security.

Foreign policy at this time was fiercely anti-colonial. Sukarno objected strongly to the fact that the British, without consulting him, established neighbouring Malaysia as an independent federation; he saw this as neo-colonialist encirclement. At the same time, however, he was having to court the favour of the world powers. As relations with the USA worsened, he turned first to the Soviets and then to China for financial support and military resources, incurring large burdens of foreign debt in the process.

The only notable challenge to Guided Democracy came from the Communist Party (PKI). After years of economic decline and unemployment, and the continuation of feudal relations on the land, people could see no visible benefit from independence. In the early 1960s drought and famine ravaged the countryside, and PKI membership grew rapidly, until it was the largest Communist Party outside the eastern bloc.

1965 – the Year of Living Dangerously

The events of 1965/6 are shrouded in mystery and rumour. The full story will perhaps never be known, but the repercussions have been felt in Indonesia ever since. On 1 October 1965, six senior generals were kidnapped and murdered by middle-ranking officers. Major-General Suharto, now the highest-ranking officer, led a successful counter-coup operation. Both the PKI and Sukarno were blamed for the plot: the communists for having planned the assassinations, and Sukarno for having done nothing to prevent them gaining so much influence. This is the official version of events, and one widely accepted by Indonesians at the time. Many academics have speculated about the possible involvement of Suharto himself in orchestrating the coup, and about the role of foreign powers in preventing the growth of communism in Indonesia.

In the months following the attempted coup, an unprecedented frenzy of violence swept the country as military and militias rounded up, tortured, and executed suspected communists. It is estimated that perhaps 500,000 people died. Hundreds of thousands more were imprisoned without trial. Former US diplomats and intelligence agents have since confirmed that the US Central Intelligence Agency supplied a list of 5000 PKI members to the Indonesian armed forces; many were summarily executed. The trauma of these ghastly events continues to haunt Indonesia.

Riding high on the wave of anti-communist feeling, and claiming to offer an alternative to political chaos and economic mismanagement, Suharto gradually gained ground, effectively taking over power from Sukarno on 11 March 1966. The old order was finished; what was soon known as the New Order had begun.

▼ Police at a political demonstration. During the Suharto years, rallies like this one were often brutally suppressed.

Suharto's New Order

Between 1966 and 1998, Indonesia had stability: one national ideology, one president, one ruling party, very little social unrest, and a growing economy. The price paid by ordinary Indonesians for this stability became increasingly heavy as the years went by.

VIOLENCE AND RESISTANCE IN ACEH

The roots of the conflict in Aceh go back to the colonial period. Aceh was fiercely resistant to Dutch rule, maintaining its independence into the early twentieth century, and continuing intermittent opposition to the colonists until the outbreak of the Second World War. An important element in the independence struggle, strongly Islamic Aceh was disappointed by the secular nature of the new republic. Under the New Order, this disaffection with Jakarta turned to outright hostility, as central government took control of Aceh's considerable natural resources, leaving the province neglected and under-developed. It is estimated that Aceh contributes around 11 per cent of the national budget, while receiving barely one per cent in return.

The separatist Free Aceh Movement – Gerakan Aceh Merdeka (GAM) – was formed in 1976. It had links with other 'liberation' movements around the world, with particularly strong support from Libya, and enjoyed considerable sympathy from the Acehnese population as a whole. The military quelled the insurgency, but GAM resurfaced in 1989, this time with a stronger Islamic character, which won it greater support from the influential religious leadership. In response, the Indonesian government designated Aceh a Region of Military Operation (Daerah Operasi Militer – DOM). This status was to remain until 1998. The government refused to recognise the political aspects of the conflict, referring to the rebels as criminal gangs.

Under DOM, the military pursued a kind of shock therapy, designed to terrify the population into ending their support for the separatists. Tactics included curfews and checkpoints, mass arrests and heavy surveillance, and raids on the houses of suspected rebels and their families. There were widespread reports of torture and killings. Several mass graves were exposed by grieving relatives in 1998.

The 1970s witnessed a programme of increasingly repressive legislation, designed to reduce the scope for political organisation. Suharto introduced an alternative to political parties: the 'functional group', Golongan Karya, known as Golkar, a government-sponsored coalition of interest groups and labour unions. Opposition parties were forced to merge into either the United Development Party (PPP), or the Indonesian Democracy Party (PDI). Party political activity and election campaigns were strictly controlled. A series of student protests in the 1970s was swiftly suppressed, and the mass media were heavily censored. By the 1980s Suharto had effectively crushed all opposition to his rule. Those who did dissent, or who were suspected of doing so, risked arrest and detention, often without trial, in one of the prison camps dotted about the archipelago.

The military – the other arm of government

The mainstay of New Order power was its close relationship with the military, made possible through the principle of *dwi fungsi,* or dual function, giving the armed forces a role in politics as well as in security. But the involvement of the military extended even beyond politics: army business interests were estimated in 1999 to be worth US$ 8 billion, with considerable stakes in the paper and pulp industry, logging, and oil refining. These figures do not include income from the army's huge private protection racket, nor the suspected illegal trade in small arms. It is estimated that 70 to 80 per cent of military income comes from non-budget sources – a fact which helps to explain many examples of military partisanship, evident either through active discrimination and abuse of power, or through omission – by failure to act to protect civilians, especially, but not exclusively, in Aceh and East Timor.

Corruption by franchise

Since the days of the Japanese occupation, corruption and graft had plagued the government, bureaucracy, and military. Beginning with Suharto himself, the New Order elevated this to a new level, with systematic and all-pervasive corruption creating a parallel 'shadow State', where licences and concessions were awarded, judicial decisions made, and promotions obtained in return for bribes.

Just as centralised government reached right down to village level, so did State-sponsored corruption. Suharto effectively granted 'franchises' to his deputies, to continue the monopoly-privileges racket at lower levels. Graft, too extended through the ranks, again with the greatest involvement at the top: Ibu Tien, Suharto's wife, was so deeply involved in graft that she was dubbed Ibu Tien Per Cent! The wealthy and well connected could operate with near impunity, fearing nothing from either government or the courts. Corruption is so deeply embedded in the Indonesian bureaucratic system that it is seen by many as an acceptable way of conducting business. Ibu Dewi, a small trader from Jakarta, comments: *'It's OK to get rich by stealing money from government budgets, but it's not OK to steal a chicken in order to eat. How can that be right?'* As a result, people's trust in government officials has been eroded to nothing.

▲ *A gas explosion lights up the night sky in Java. Concessions granted to business associates of the former regime meant that local people often failed to benefit from the exploitation of natural resources, and now they suffer the consequences of the resulting pollution.*

Relations with the outside world

The New Order was a friend of the West during the Cold War, providing an important buttress against the threatened advance of communism from East Asia. When the Cold War ended, globalisation took its place as the driving force of international relations, linking the world's economies closer than ever before. Suharto assumed, apparently correctly, that he could continue to enjoy economic support, irrespective of political and human-rights considerations. Foreign investment and aid were readily forthcoming throughout the New Order period. Neither the international financial institutions nor foreign governments had any desire to see Indonesia's economic bubble burst; thus they were willing to continue to overlook the abuses of Suharto's authoritarian regime, in the interests of economic stability. This strategic significance gave Indonesia substantial immunity from external criticism of its domestic human-rights record. The forcible annexation of East Timor in 1975 was carried out with the knowledge and tacit acceptance of Western leaders. This history of unaccountability means that the international community now has limited leverage to influence the Indonesian government.

New Order centralism: stifling local initiative

The Indonesian State under the New Order was strongly centralised. All policy was controlled by central departments in Jakarta. As policy was formulated in Java, there was a tendency for programmes to reflect Javanese priorities, agricultural practices, and political structures, rather than taking account of regional variations. Many of the civil servants posted to regional offices were also Javanese, leading to a growing sense of 'Javanisation' in the provinces, and a resentment of and alienation from government programmes.

This system of top–down, uniform government has had some far-reaching effects. First, it facilitated the endemic corruption that plagues the Indonesian bureaucracy. Poorly paid civil servants depend on additional income from a cycle of institutionalised bribery which is difficult for an individual to break. Second, the lack of opportunity for local decision-making means that neither local officials nor citizens have a stake in making a success of policies imposed from above. Indonesia is littered with failed government-sponsored development schemes, which at best are a waste of time and money, and at worst actually undermine existing local initiatives. Third, heavily centralised revenue and taxation systems meant that resource-rich areas such as West Papua remained impoverished, as income from mining and oil exploitation went straight to Jakarta, before being redistributed to regional public institutions. Central government prioritised national development rather than the sustainable management of natural resources, with the result that local people had to stand by helplessly while their environment was threatened through over-exploitation, the profits of which would not benefit the community.

The New Order deliberately cultivated passive, obedient citizens, who accepted whatever unsolicited subsidy or project came their way. Because there was no opportunity to contribute to the policy-making process, or share in local decision making, community organisations were seriously weakened. A whole generation of disempowerment has undermined local people's capacity to challenge authority or to take the initiative to improve their lives.

Pembangunan: a better life through building

The New Order saw development (*pembangunan*, which also means 'construction') as its mission. In 1966 Indonesia was one of the poorest countries in the world; between 1966 and 1995 per capita income quadrupled, mainly thanks to the oil boom of the 1970s. The New Order carried out some ambitious social policies, mainly emphasising visible infrastructure.

Health care

A network of primary health-care centres was established across the country, supported by 250,000 health clinics at village level. The scale of this operation was impressive, but health services were spread rather thinly, and the standard of care was often low. By the mid-1990s many people had rejected the government services in favour of treatment by traditional practitioners, which was cheaper and offered better quality. Despite these problems, infant mortality fell from 124 per thousand live births in 1967 to 47 in 1997, although the rate is still far higher than Malaysia's, where the comparable figure is nine. It also disguises significant regional variations: the rate in Jakarta is less than half that in the eastern islands of Nusa Tenggara. Similarly, impressive advances have been made in reducing maternal mortality rates, but they remain shockingly high in some areas.

One initiative which looks impressive on paper is the family-planning programme. Although the population of Indonesia doubled between 1969 and 1999, fertility rates were halved, and the rate of population growth fell significantly during this time. This was achieved through a countrywide programme of education and persuasion, promoting a range of contraceptive methods. Indonesia was widely praised by the international community for the extraordinary success of this initiative.

In some areas, however, there are suggestions that project workers, anxious to meet demanding targets, gave inadequate information to participants and coerced, rather than persuaded, people (usually women) to 'accept' family planning.

▼ *'Two children are enough.' Statues promoting family planning in Bali use a traditional style to portray a small family, looking prosperous and happy.*

Reports from West Papua and East Timor suggest that family planning has been used as a means of limiting the growth of 'troublesome' populations. In West Papua, in an area identified for extensive mining operations, and as a major transmigration site, indigenous populations were targeted for family-planning schemes to a greater degree than transmigrant communities. It was reported that women were being bribed to accept contraception, and that extensive use was being made of long-term injectable contraceptives. In East Timor, an independent report presented evidence that women were being covertly sterilised during routine surgical operations, and that in the late 1980s young women were given compulsory long-term contraceptive injections.

Education: quantity not quality

Between 1973 and 1979, Indonesia built 61,000 primary schools – one of the world's most dramatic expansions in elementary education. In 1984 primary education became compulsory, and rates for primary-school enrolment now stand at 95 per cent. The levels of school enrolment for boys and girls are roughly equal. Despite these impressive figures, 20 per cent of children do not finish primary school. Although school fees are fairly insignificant, families have to find extra money for uniforms, books, and substantial 'voluntary' contributions to the school.

▼ *Primary-school children in Sumba. Compulsory uniform is a heavy additional expense for poorer families.*

Even for those who can afford it, the quality of teaching and learning is often poor. Indonesia spent only 1.7 per cent of its GDP on education in 1997, less than half the allocation in neighbouring Malaysia. Teacher training is of a low standard, and books and materials are scarce. The teaching style is often very formal, and the national curriculum is old-fashioned, with a strong emphasis on academic skills, which lack relevance for many young people.

K H Nuruddin A Rahman runs an Islamic boarding school in Madura, an island off the east coast of Java. He argues that the State education system does not nurture the individual talents and interests of the child, or provide moral guidance. '*It is simply intended to instil knowledge in order to develop the country*', he says. '*This is teaching, and not education. Children become clever, but not good, and the country has suffered as a result.*' Education is seen as a way of raising social status, rather than a vehicle for personal, intellectual, and moral development. The system perpetuates the idea that occupations such as farming and trading are for those who fail to get a desk job in the civil service.

Transmigration

Jatibali is a village just outside Kendari in South-East Sulawesi, but you would be forgiven for thinking otherwise. Inhabitants have Balinese names, look Balinese, and speak Balinese. Hindu temples strewn with brightly coloured offerings of fruit and flowers line the streets, and the smell of incense hangs in the air. But something about the village doesn't feel quite right. The streets are arranged on an uncharacteristically regular grid system, and instead of the traditional Balinese family compounds, with a high wall surrounding a group of buildings, the houses are set facing the road in individual plots. This isn't Bali: this is a transmigration site.

Indonesia's population is very unevenly distributed. Fifty-nine per cent of the population lives on Java, which makes up only seven per cent of the landmass. The Dutch began a system of government-sponsored migration in the early twentieth century, called 'colonisation'. The independent Indonesian government continued this policy, renaming it 'transmigration'. It is estimated that between 1950 and 1990 more than six million people were relocated, either at government expense or as self-funded migrants. Transmigration had three overt goals: reducing population pressure in Java and Bali; aiding poverty reduction by enabling transmigrants to establish more prosperous livelihoods; and contributing to regional development.

Jatibali was one of the first New Order settlements, established in 1968. One hundred and fifty Balinese families were offered the chance to move to Sulawesi; they were promised housing, two hectares of land, and a year's worth of rice and medicine. When they arrived, the site was covered in scrub, and accommodation was very poor. '*It was a difficult few years*', explains I Wayan Cengker, who was a small boy when his family arrived.

▲ I. Wayan Cengker in the garden of his home in the transmigration village of Jatibali, near Kendari in South-East Sulawesi. Behind him stand the family altars that are characteristic of Balinese Hinduism.

'The food we were given was not nearly enough – our family's monthly allocation was usually finished within a week, and we were very hungry. The land we had been given had been used as a military zone by the Japanese during the war. The fields were strewn with bullets and unexploded ordnance, and several children were injured.' Relations with the local people were not easy at first, and the new arrivals were viewed with suspicion. 'We would have gone home if we could', recalls Pak Wayan.

Thirty years on, things are rather different. By the 1980s the farms of the transmigrants began to thrive. Relations with local people also improved: 'Now we share the work at harvest time.' Residents have improved their houses, and built temples. 'Of course we miss our family in Bali,' says Pak Wayan, 'but we stay in touch, and visit when we can. The most important thing for us is to have a secure livelihood.'

Not such a good idea

Not all transmigration stories have such a happy ending. By the 1980s, with substantial financial support from the World Bank and other bilateral donors, the programme was scaled up considerably. Many later transmigration sites were cleared from forest land, more suited to the cultivation of tubers and vegetables, combined with long fallow periods, than to the intensive irrigated rice production that Javanese and Balinese transmigrants were used to. Conditions were often extremely poor; some sources cite a 40–50 per cent rate of return, as families abandoned efforts to make a living.

For those who remained, relations with local people were often decidedly hostile, as poor crop yields often forced transmigrants to seek off-farm employment, and therefore compete with locals for jobs. There were increasing concerns about the exploitation of the environment, as more land was cleared for transmigrant settlements. In 1991 transmigration was estimated to be the single most important cause of deforestation, resulting in the loss of 1.2 million hectares of forest each year. Indigenous people were often forced to surrender customarily owned land to transmigrants, without proper compensation, and concerns were raised about the disproportionate number of transmigrants resettled in areas with a strong separatist movement, such as Aceh and West Papua. This served only to increase the suspicion of outer-island inhabitants that transmigration was simply another method of extending Java's control over the provinces. On top of all this, there is no evidence that transmigration was an effective poverty-reduction strategy, or that it did anything to alleviate population pressure on Java and Bali.

The programme was suspended in 2000, partly on grounds of expense (it costs around US$ 7000 to move a family and support it for a year), and partly owing to increased opposition to the policy, both inside and outside the country. In view of the new powers given to regional government, it is unlikely that the programme will be reinstated in its original guise. There are, however, fears that transmigration could reappear in the form of refugee resettlement. Meanwhile, many millions of families like Wayan Cengker's continue to try to make a new home from home for themselves.

An end in sight?

After the end of the Cold War in 1989, the New Order faced increasing international pressure to improve its records on conservation of the environment and respect for human rights. But as long as the economy continued to do well, and foreign investment seemed secure, the government could largely ignore criticism from outside. There was little sign that the regime was about to crumble. But the economy did not continue to grow. From the middle of 1997 there began a series of events which would lead to economic disaster and political crisis. The age of stability was over.

The economy in crisis

▼ The economic crisis hit urban communities hardest, leaving many people out of work – like these men in a poor district of Yogyakarta.

Of all the countries which suffered in the Asian financial crisis of the late 1990s, Indonesia was the worst affected. Between November 1997 and July 1998, the *rupiah* fell to one-sixth of its previous value, inflation was running at 68 per cent, and the economy shrank by 14 per cent, taking it back to 1994 levels. Yet the crisis did not affect people as severely as first predicted. As much as the government social safety-net programmes, it was Indonesians' extended family networks and general resourcefulness that helped to protect individuals from complete destitution.

Background to the crisis

Until the mid-1990s, Indonesia was seen as one of the 'Asian tiger' economies, with an annual growth rate of around seven per cent a year, inflation below ten per cent, and a healthy export sector, featuring manufactured goods and oil, gas, and minerals. General living standards in the country rose steadily in the 1980s and 1990s. However, this state of affairs had a fatal flaw. Although, compared with some developing countries, wealth in Indonesia was relatively evenly spread, a small economic elite, closely linked to the government, was able to finance many of its ventures with unsecured loans from State banks. This cosy relationship was not easily open to outside inspection and eventually, inevitably, it fostered a corrupt system of crony capitalism.

Corruption and cronyism did not cause the economic collapse, although they meant that its effects were more far-reaching. In Indonesia, as in the other Asian tiger economies, rapid development was sustained not by domestic savings and investments, but by huge inputs of foreign capital, which were always liable to be withdrawn. In reality, the 'economic success story' was based more on wishful thinking than on sound financial practice.

The crunch comes

In the Thailand of the 1990s, foreign investment took the form of high levels of short-term borrowing and property speculation. In May 1997 investors, responding to the unsustainable rate of borrowing in the Thai economy, began pulling capital out of the country. Currency speculators, seeing the unstable state of the Thai *baht*, quickly moved in, and the currency collapsed. By July the *rupiah* began to follow suit, as foreign investors took fright and removed their capital from the Indonesian money market. In late October the International Monetary Fund (IMF) announced a rescue package worth US$ 43 billion over three years, composed of pledges from other Asian countries, the World Bank, and the IMF itself. The money came with conditions. These included rapid reform of the banking sector, an improvement in the balance of trade, and an opening of Indonesian markets to foreign competition.

In response to the IMF's demands, 16 failing banks were closed immediately, causing a run on the remaining banks as people rushed to withdraw their savings. The IMF has since admitted that it was wrong to demand this action. In the months that followed, President Suharto was reluctant to agree to the remaining conditions, the economic crisis deepened, and the country was thrown into political turmoil. In early 1998 food riots swept the country, in protest against huge price rises. The *rupiah* continued to fall, from around Rp2500 to the dollar in mid-1997 to a low of Rp17,000, before stabilising at around Rp9000, where it remained in mid-2002.

▶ A mother brings her baby for immunisation. Clinics like this one, run by volunteers for displaced people resettled on the island of Buton, suffered as a result of the economic crisis.

What effect did it have?

The effects of the crisis, known as Krismon (*krisis moneter* – monetary crisis), were felt most keenly in urban areas. It is difficult to know precisely how many people lost their jobs, as there is no social welfare system in Indonesia, and therefore the register of the unemployed is highly inaccurate. Workers in textile and footwear factories, the majority of whom are women, as well as those in the construction and automotive industries, suffered heavy job losses. Prices for basic goods such as rice, kerosene (used as a cooking fuel), and petrol rose sharply, because the government was unable to continue subsidising them. The surge in inflation in mid-1998 affected food prices most of all.

In 1998 the average Indonesian family saw ten years of savings wiped out in six months. With no reserves to fall back on, it became harder for poor urban families to afford essentials such as medicines and school fees. There is evidence of a decline in the standards of child and maternal health, especially in poor urban communities. The proportion of children using government health services fell from 26 per cent in 1997 to 20 per cent in 1999, which affected levels of preventative care, for example immunisation programmes and vitamin distribution. Despite efforts to prevent children dropping out of school, there was a clear decline in school enrolments, especially in the numbers of children making the transition from primary to junior high school. Women and girls tended to be worst affected, with girls often leaving school and marrying very early.

Despite the hardship, early estimates suggesting that half of Indonesia's population would fall below the poverty line proved to be exaggerated. At least in the early months of the crisis, job losses in urban areas were matched by increases in rural employment, as families absorbed relatives from the cities. The proportion of the population living in poverty was probably nearer 25 to 30 per cent, although the gap between the very rich and the very poor grew wider. Many more people, though not at the point of total destitution, became much more vulnerable to unexpected disasters such as illness or failed harvests, as the crisis forced them to exhaust their savings and sell off non-essential assets.

Ibu Muriah has a stall selling cold drinks and snacks at Taman Mini theme park in Jakarta. She was a full-time housewife until 2000, when the strain of raising three children on her husband's civil-service salary became too much for the family. *'Government salaries have not kept pace with inflation,'* Ibu Muriah explains, *'so our household needed an extra income. It's hard to make ends meet when you need to buy books and school uniforms, and pay for transport. The price rises have made life very difficult for women trying to balance the household budget.'*

The government responded to the rising levels of poverty with an emergency welfare programme known as 'the social safety net'. The most important element was the provision of heavily subsidised rice for the poorest families, but it also included education scholarships, some health subsidies, and a job-creation scheme which paid people to do labour-intensive work such as street cleaning. This was the first time the State had provided welfare benefits of this kind, and the scheme has continued and developed since 1998. In 2002 the Social Compensation Fund, as it is now known, had a budget of Rp800 billion, subsidising health

▼ *Although women have always played an important role in the Indonesian economy, the crisis forced more of them to seek paid work. Many established small food-stalls like this one in Blora, Central Java.*

The currency devaluation effectively quadrupled the value of Indonesia's foreign debt, and the IMF loans only added to it. The result was that from March 1998 to March 2000 the national debt increased from 23 per cent of gross domestic product to a massive 91 per cent. Since then, there has been much discussion about the level of influence exerted by the IMF, the World Bank, and other international creditors and donors over Indonesian economic policy. The need to speed up economic recovery in order to service this huge debt has led to reductions in the social budget, with reduced resources for health and education. It has also put added pressure on government to allow unrestricted exploitation of natural resources, in order to boost the balance of payments. Agreeing to overseas donors' demands can cause tension at home. President Wahid faced popular protest when he cut government subsidies on basic goods like petrol in order to meet IMF requirements.

and education services for poor families. Critics of the scheme say that it is very difficult to ensure that the fund reaches the poorest people, and that such a large amount of money would be better used for developing long-term strategies to lift people out of poverty.

Fighting back: the informal sector

Many city workers, made redundant as a result of the economic crisis, were reduced to making a living as self-employed casual traders. The fallout from the economic crisis has enlarged and enlivened an already thriving informal economy in urban Indonesia.

M Abadi Datuk Kinali used to work in the marketing department of a textile company in Jakarta. With the onset of the economic crisis in 1997, the firm went bankrupt and he lost his job. Seeing little chance of being re-employed in the formal sector as the crisis deepened, he and his wife moved to Yogyakarta. Like many others left unemployed by the crisis, Pak Datuk began work as a *klithikan*, an informal trader of second-hand goods. He has a stall in the impromptu flea market which, since the crisis, has sprung up every afternoon on Jalan Mangkubumi, a busy shopping street in central Yogyakarta, where he sells a variety of household

▶ Police in Surabaya raid the mobile stalls of informal street vendors. Often the only way for small traders to avoid this kind of treatment is to pay bribes.

KRISMON? YES PLEASE!

The collapse of the *rupiah* was not bad news for everybody in Indonesia. Export-oriented businesses actually benefited from the poor exchange rate — even smaller enterprises, which are usually more susceptible to economic instability. The furniture industry in Jepara in Central Java, for example, which is dominated by small businesses producing for overseas markets, actually continued to grow during the crisis. In rural areas, too, the effects were mixed. Although inflation meant rising prices, farmers who were producing crops for export, such as copra, coffee, and cocoa, found their cash incomes rising even faster. Those who also continued to grow most of their staple food were even better insulated against local price rises for basic goods. There were reports that sales of electrical goods such as televisions and refrigerators actually rose in parts of Sulawesi during 1998.

and electronic goods — anything he can get his hands on. *Klithikan* are just one type of informal trader, running businesses from wooden stalls with wheels, called *kaki lima*, or 'five feet' (if you count two wheels and a stand, as well as the trader's own, it makes sense!). Other *kaki lima* sell food or drink, or sweets and cigarettes and other everyday goods. They can be seen everywhere in Indonesian towns. Pak Datuk says the *klithikan* are a good example of the way in which *wong cilik*, or 'small people', have responded creatively to the pressures of the economic crisis, while providing a useful service. *'The presence of the* klithikan *makes an area more bustling, and therefore safer for inhabitants. Also people can buy all kinds of goods at reasonable prices.'*

Signs of recovery?

In general, recovery from the crisis has been slow. Although the confidence of international investors is slowly returning, life is still difficult for many poor families. Real wages fell sharply and have only partly recovered, and prices of basic goods, especially kerosene and petrol, are still rising, as Indonesia struggles to combat the effects of years of subsidy and lift prices up to the level of world markets, as demanded by the World Bank and the IMF. Predictions are beginning to sound more positive, although there will be no speedy return to the dramatic growth rates of the 1980s and early 1990s.

Reformasi and after

'*Reformasi* toll road', Kendari, South-East Sulawesi

It is early 1998. The economy is in crisis, inflation is out of control, and riots are sweeping the country. Still, President Suharto clings to power, and Golkar nominates him as its candidate for a seventh term in office. By May, angry students are demonstrating outside Parliament in Jakarta, demanding Suharto's resignation, political *reformasi* (reform), and an end to 'corruption, collusion, and nepotism'. They are joined by poor urban workers, hit hard by the economic crisis. On 12 May four students from Trisakti University in Jakarta are shot dead by security forces, following a peaceful demonstration. The shootings precipitate mass riots, with hundreds of thousands of people out on the streets in cities all over Indonesia. Finally, on 21 May, Suharto is forced out of office. A regime which lasted 32 years has finally fallen, and now everything will change.

Or will it? Since the euphoria of mid-1998, Indonesia has seen some dramatic changes, but in many ways the fundamental structures of the

► A demonstration in support of reformasi. Young people, especially university students, were at the forefront of the street protests in 1998.

political, economic, and judicial systems remain basically unaltered. There are some encouraging signs. Parliament, taking its representative role seriously for the first time, is starting to find its critical voice in debates about government policy. The liberated media and an energetic non-government sector have enlivened political and social debate. On the other hand, many prominent figures from New Order days remain in influential positions, and the pervasive collusion between the bureaucracy, the army, and the private sector is unchanged. Ordinary Indonesians, frustrated by the slow pace of change, see little improvement in their daily lives.

Habibie: riding the wave of reform

When Suharto resigned and his Vice-President took over the leadership, few people expected it to remain in his hands for long. B J Habibie, a German-educated aeronautical engineer, was viewed as an unreconstructed New Order man, unlikely to bring about the radical change that people were demanding. In fact, he remained in power for 17 months, and, swept along by the momentum of the *reformasi* movement, presided over some important pieces of reforming legislation.

Under Habibie, electoral laws were reformed to allow multi-party elections. As part of these changes to the formal political system, the huge power of the President was restricted, and the military's representation in Parliament was reduced. Habibie's government also rescinded some of the more repressive labour laws, relaxing the restrictions on the right of association and the freedom of the press, and released political prisoners. New laws on regional autonomy were drafted.

East Timor's painful parting

Perhaps the most unexpected event of Habibie's interregnum was his declaration, in January 1999, that the East Timorese should be offered a referendum to decide whether they wished to remain part of Indonesia. East Timor, a former Portuguese colony, had begun a process of decolonisation after Portugal itself democratised in 1974. In 1975 the country was invaded by Indonesian troops, and the following year was officially annexed as the Republic's twenty-seventh province. Although the annexation was never recognised by the United Nations, no determined action was taken, either by the Portuguese, or by the international community as a whole, to repulse the Indonesian offensive. A guerrilla resistance movement, later led by Xanana Gusmao, survived in the East Timorese mountains throughout the occupation. By 1999, Gusmao had been in prison in Jakarta for seven years. In 1996 the exiled East Timorese Minister for External Affairs, Jose Ramos Horta, and Carlos Belo, Bishop of East Timor, shared the Nobel Prize for Peace.

Habibie's announcement was a calculated gamble. If Indonesia won the referendum, the world would recognise East Timor's incorporation into Indonesia. But the risk of failure was considerable. All senior generals had invested much of their careers in the East Timorese campaign (not to mention the considerable assets held by New Order military and political figures in East Timor). The military also feared that if East Timor achieved independence, this would set a dangerous precedent for other regions with secessionist aspirations, including Papua and Aceh, and lead to general national disintegration. In East Timor, life under Indonesian occupation was marked by violence and fear, which only increased in the months leading up to the referendum, as integrationist militia, organised, armed, and encouraged by the Indonesian military, undertook a campaign of disruption and intimidation, causing the ballot to be postponed twice. The Indonesian government refused to allow a UN peace-keeping force into the territory, and remained responsible for maintaining security.

On 30 August 1999, the East Timorese voted overwhelmingly in favour of independence. Immediately the result was announced, the pro-Indonesia militia embarked on an obviously pre-planned programme of violence and destruction. Thousands of buildings were destroyed; citizens were raped, terrorised, and murdered, the UN compound was besieged, and tens of thousands of people fled or were forcibly evacuated over the border to camps in West Timor. A specially formed UN force eventually regained control of East Timor. However, pro-integration militia, only partially disbanded and disarmed by Indonesian troops, continue to control the West Timor refugee camps where, by mid-2002, an estimated 50,000 East Timorese remained trapped. There is a widespread feeling that the failure to protect the rights of East Timorese refugees was a failing of both the Indonesian government and the United Nations.

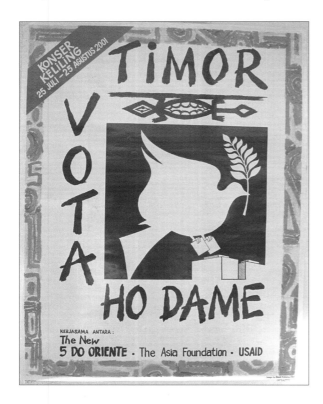

▼ *East Timor, August 2001: a poster urging people to vote in the election for a new government*

In April 2002, Xanana Gusmao was elected as President of an independent East Timor. At the same time, 18 leading figures allegedly involved in the shocking events in East Timor, including Abilio Soares, the former Governor, and Timbul Silaen, the former Chief of Police, went on trial in Jakarta. At a specially established tribunal, the men were charged with failing to keep the peace in East Timor. Many, including Silaen, were acquitted. Soares was jailed for only three years for abusing human rights. The trials have been criticised by many observers, including the United Nations. Many view them as an elaborate farce, designed to satisfy US conditions for a resumption of military links, and to stave off calls for an international tribunal.

► *A street mural depicts the presidents of Indonesia; from right to left: Sukarno, Suharto, B.J. Habibie, Abdurrahman Wahid, and Megawati Sukarnoputri.*

Wahid: civil society takes the lead

In June 1999 some 112 million Indonesians voted in the first democratic elections since 1955. Forty-eight parties participated. The Democratic Party of Struggle (PDI-P), led by Megawati Sukarnoputri, the daughter of Sukarno, the first President of the Republic, won the largest share of the vote, followed by Golkar. In October, members of the People's Consultative Assembly voted for the new president. The election was won not by Megawati, but by Abdurrahman Wahid, known affectionately as Gus Dur, the respected cleric and leader of the country's largest Muslim organisation, *Nahdlatul Ulama*. Megawati was elected as his Vice-President, and it was hoped that this partnership would unite the anti-Golkar movement and provide a stable platform for continued reform.

Gus Dur's eccentric approach to politics won him both admirers and enemies. His supporters hailed him as the wise fool, out-manoeuvring his opponents with his wily approach. His position as a moderate Muslim who vigorously defended Indonesia's religious pluralism, yet remained a respected figure in the Islamic world, was particularly valuable. Critics claimed that he often contradicted himself and was fond of making announcements without consulting his cabinet. Added to this, his poor health – he suffered a serious stroke in 1998, and is almost blind – was a cause for concern. Nevertheless, he did continue the programme of reform, relaxing some of the restrictions on Chinese Indonesians, and, controversially, proposing to lift the ban on communism. He also further loosened the army's grip on political power.

Wahid's challenge to the power of the military eventually contributed to his downfall. As time went on, even those who had at first welcomed Gus Dur as President began to feel disenchanted with his performance. He was accused of involvement in a corruption scandal involving the State logistics agency. After a series of increasingly desperate exchanges with Parliament, he was finally impeached by a special sitting of the upper house in July 2001, on the grounds of corruption and incompetence. His place was taken by the Vice-President, Megawati.

Megawati: her father's daughter

Megawati's lineage as the daughter of President Sukarno has guaranteed her status as a popular symbol of resistance. Her political vision is very simple, and strongly reminiscent of that of her father: a unified, democratic Indonesian nation-state, with no concessions to separatists. In stark contrast with Wahid, she rarely gives interviews or makes political speeches. Critics have interpreted her silence as evidence of her lack of understanding of the political environment; her supporters claim that the maternal figurehead is actually a shrewd team player.

Under Megawati, Indonesia remains one of the most corrupt countries in the world. Some progress has been made in recent years: there is more reporting of corruption, and a number of high-profile cases have recently come to trial. Akbar Tanjung, Golkar Chairman and Speaker of the House of Representatives, was arrested in March 2002, accused of embezzling nearly US$ 4 million from the State logistics agency in 1999. He allegedly used the funds to finance Golkar's election campaign. At the same time, Indonesia was following the progress of the trial of Hutomo 'Tommy' Mandala Putra, son of former President Suharto, accused of involvement in the murder of the judge who presided over his own corruption trial.

Independent watchdog agencies, such as Indonesia Corruption Watch, are playing an important part in monitoring government activity, and holding it accountable for abuses. But such agencies are powerless unless their investigations are backed up by an independent and competent judiciary. There is still suspicion that many recent high-level prosecutions were motivated by political rather than judicial priorities. Several senior bank and government officials who have been investigated on corruption charges since 2000 have escaped heavy sentences. For ordinary people, however, taking a grievance to court is an expensive process, unlikely to result in success; a popular saying in Indonesia warns: '*Report a lost chicken, and in the end you lose a goat too*'.

▼ *Student demonstration on the streets of Jakarta, March 2002: the Pinocchio mask, symbolising lies and corruption, lampoons the Parliamentary Speaker, Akbar Tanjung.*

Power to the regions: opportunities ...

Regional autonomy may not sound like the most revolutionary or controversial concept, but its implications for local democracy and accountable government are among the most hotly debated issues in Indonesia today. Under new laws, passed in 1999 and implemented in 2001, considerable power is devolved to elected regional parliaments; each in turn elects its own leader, the Bupati. Only fiscal policy, the judiciary, religious matters, and defence and foreign policy are reserved for central government. A new system of revenue sharing has altered the financial relationship between central and local government, with more locally raised revenue remaining in local hands.

Although the legislation on local autonomy was drafted rather hastily and has some serious flaws, many people are optimistic about the new system, especially those who were on the receiving end of some of Jakarta's misjudged development schemes. Nuruddin A Rahman is a teacher and senior religious figure in Madura. He feels that Madura has been ignored by Jakarta and left behind by the rest of Indonesia in terms of development: *'The people of Madura have become spectators'*, he says. Central government was good at building things that people did not actually want: physical construction projects which did not improve the general standard of living. Instead, what is needed is sympathetic development which does not destroy the local culture and environment. Pak Nuruddin explains: *'Build up Madura, don't build in Madura. Regional autonomy ought to help people to refuse things they don't want.'*

Autonomy should also help people to attain things that they do want. Under the new legislation, responsibility for education is devolved to local government. There is a basic compulsory national curriculum, but this is kept to a minimum, to allow for regional variety and the inclusion of practical skills-training. Regional languages are finding their way on to the school timetable. In Wonosobo, in central Java, a syllabus which includes material on conservation and forest management is being introduced, to coincide with local government legislation which transfers the responsibility for maintaining forest lands to local people. It is hoped that this will make education more relevant and stimulating for Indonesia's children.

There is widespread support, too, for the closer link between revenue raised in a region, and local government spending power. People also hope that, by making local government directly accountable to a local electorate, the process of governance will become more transparent and less open to corruption. It could also help to restore public confidence in government if popular local figures with strong support are elected. K H Imam Buchori Kholil AG is standing as a candidate for Bupati in Bangkalan, in Madura. If he wins, this will unite elected, traditional, and religious authority, because he is descended from a line of revered local scholars and leaders, as well as being the local chairman of the Islamic organisation *Nahdlatul Ulama*. *'People in Madura recognise the authority of their father, their religious teachers, and the government, in that order,'* says Pak Nuruddin. A combination of all three, then, might be what is needed to lend government some long-overdue legitimacy.

... and threats

On the less positive side, there are concerns that regional autonomy will simply transfer problems of corruption and inefficiency to the local level, with regional leaders establishing powerful personal fiefdoms, and the benefits of local control over revenue extending only to a small elite. In some areas, regional politicians have voted themselves substantial pay rises, and have benefited from expensive overseas trips – not the kind of activity guaranteed to inspire the confidence of a sceptical electorate.

Others worry that regional autonomy will increase the chances of tension between natives of an area and newcomers. Ethno-centrism has become increasingly evident in several areas since 1998. It is feared that local government could come to mean ethnic government, discriminating against Indonesians from other areas. Indeed, there have been reports in some regions of non-indigenous people being excluded from civil-service positions.

More generally, there has been a concern that neither government nor electorate were properly prepared for the handover of power, which has left some local authorities floundering, and many citizens uncertain about the role of the new institutions. Critics claim that the mechanisms for delivering this new empowerment remain obscure, and people have been left with high expectations of a prosperous future, but only a vague sense of how this could be achieved.

Regional autonomy is clearly not a panacea which will cure all of Indonesia's problems. It does have real potential for rebuilding trust in government, and enabling local participation in decision making, but if this opportunity is abused by local figures seeking power on the same terms as the New Order, the consequences could be extremely damaging.

▼ *There are concerns that decentralisation could lead to increased ethnic discrimination against people such as these Butonese mothers and children, displaced from Maluku by communal conflict.*

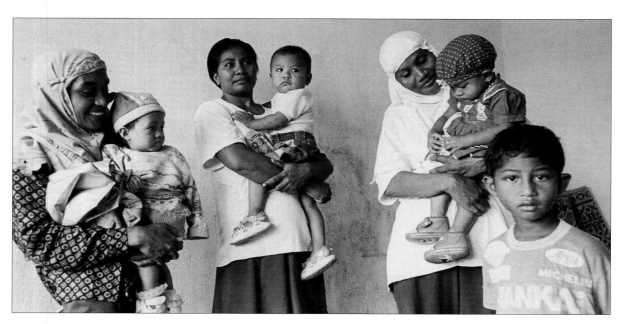

REGIONAL AUTONOMY IN AN OUT-OF-THE-WAY PLACE

The Kei islands in Maluku are on the margins of Indonesian political life. Living 2500 kilometres from Jakarta, residents of this small group of islands are used to being neglected and dictated to by central government. The Bupati (leader of the regional parliament), centrally appointed under the old system, was the focus of vigorous protests at the time of the *reformasi* demonstrations in 1998, accused of corruption and nepotism by student demonstrators.

Understandably, many people are optimistic about the new local autonomy law, and are hopeful that it will give them a greater voice in debates about how their islands are run. A local government official explains that, with more control over the budget, Kei will be able to respond to its own priorities. *'We can make more plans for the future, and can target the money where it's needed, which in Kei is to support the fishing industry, and to improve human resources. It will also mean more direct benefits for local people. For example, under the new rules, ten per cent of the income from harbour taxes collected in Tual [the capital] will have to go directly to Tual itself.'* There is also a hope that the changes will forge closer and more constructive relationships between village-government structures and the higher levels of local government, and so avoid the imposition of unwanted development projects, although it will not be easy to reverse the effects of a generation of neglect: *'Why are we being listened to only now, after being ignored for 30 years?'* asks one man, bitterly.

THE RISE OF POLITICAL ISLAM?

Islamic groups have played an important role in Indonesian politics since independence. Yet, despite being home to the largest Muslim population of any country in the world, Indonesia is not an Islamic state.

Although there has been renewed interest in religious activities over the last few years – record numbers of Indonesians are making the pilgrimage to Mecca, for example – this did not translate into electoral success for Islamic parties in the 1999 general election. The emergence of militant Islamic groups such as Laskar Jihad, sending forces to participate in conflicts between Christians and Muslims in Sulawesi and Maluku, has prompted many observers to speculate on the potential for the rise of fundamentalist Islam in Indonesia. However, these groups do not appear to enjoy much popular support among Indonesian Muslims in general (despite the evidence on the football shirt, right).

Since the events of 11 September 2001, domestic Islamic groups were angered by the US retaliation in Afghanistan, which they saw as an attack on Islam, and Megawati found herself trying to balance their concerns with the need to maintain good relations with the United States. Nevertheless, there are influential voices of moderation in Indonesian Islam. Unlike Malaysia and the Philippines, Indonesia has not so far been identified as a major centre for transnational Islamic terrorist networks.

Unity in diversity?

Difference and the Indonesian State

Indonesia's 200 million citizens represent a wealth of differing ethnic and cultural traditions. The national symbol, the mythical *garuda* bird, clasps in its claws the legend *Bhinneka Tunggal Ika* – 'unity in diversity'. Under Suharto the emphasis was placed firmly on unity (or rather conformity), at the expense of diversity. In an attempt to forge a sense of Indonesian identity, New Order nationalists went to considerable lengths to understate and depoliticise ethnic and cultural differences. It was felt that allowing free reign to ethnic expression would undermine the stability of the country. A good example of this is evident in the Taman Mini theme park in Jakarta, where various regions of the country are represented only by innocuous exhibitions of traditional costume and architecture.

The 'model' New Order Indonesian was based on an idealised view of the Javanese peasant: hardworking, God-fearing, and obedient. There were designated roles for particular sections of society: students should concern themselves with acquiring skills useful for national development (and not get involved in politics); workers should accept their employer's paternalistic role in determining their salaries, and should strike only in exceptional circumstances. Women's roles were primarily defined as wives and mothers, nurturing the next generation. Although there was nothing to prevent a woman having a career, or deciding not to marry (and women have had equal rights to vote and stand for election to Parliament since the country's independence), the social pressure to conform to this model was (and still is) strong.

Many groups, especially upland hunter-gatherers or shifting cultivators, who did not match the ideal image, were labelled backward or primitive, and lined up for 'development' – or simply ignored.

▲ *A traditional priest at a ceremony in West Sumba. Some isolated traditional communities were 'encouraged' by the New Order government to abandon their customary practices and participate in official development programmes.*

◄ *Above: A game of football in Mardika.*

Below: Friday prayers in the Al-Akbar Mosque, Surabaya

The Bajau village of Tolando, in Buton, is approached in a slightly unconventional fashion – along a 200-metre coral walkway, straight out to sea from the beach. Around 400 people live here, in wooden houses built on tall stilts above the water. The term 'Bajau' is applied to a variety of seafaring peoples who live in scattered settlements across island South-East Asia. Today only a small number of Bajau actually live in boats or 'sea houses', but small children still learn to paddle canoes almost before they can walk. *'Bajau children walk differently from their land-living schoolfriends!'*, says the village secretary.

Indonesia does not officially admit to having any indigenous peoples. Instead, it has 'isolated tribes', who, according to the government, have not yet benefited from the advantages of modernity, and need assistance to become proper citizens, through education, settled agriculture, and the acceptance of government-planned development projects. (Homosexuals, on the other hand, do not exist at all in the government's eyes. Homosexuality is not therefore illegal, and Indonesia has a thriving and distinctive, if relatively small, gay culture.)

Upland communities, while still facing considerable threats to their way of life from logging and mining companies, are beginning to make their voices heard through non-government organisations. Ethnic difference has become impossible to ignore, as inter-ethnic conflict flares in several regions. 'Unity in diversity' needs to be reinterpreted to take proper account of all sections of Indonesia's population.

Adat: living traditions

Although the government, in its concern to encourage a modern concept of citizenship, chooses not to acknowledge the differences between Indonesians, cultural diversity is alive and well. You do not need to move far from the shiny steel and glass towers of big business, or from the corridors of a government ministry, to discover that much of Indonesia lives by a set of rules and practices determined not by macro-economics or State policy, but by centuries of locally based tradition, belief, and custom.

Adat is the Indonesian term given to the hundreds of codes of traditional law and behaviour operating within the archipelago. The nature, extent, and strength of traditional practices and beliefs vary greatly. *Adat* can determine how land (or sea) is owned, distributed, and used, and can regulate the exploitation of natural resources. It can establish who is allowed to marry whom, on what terms, and how husband and wife should behave towards each other. It can also provide a community with moral guidance, and specify punishments for transgressors. *Adat* can prescribe rituals and ceremonies to mark life-cycle events and points in the agricultural calendar, or as acts of thanksgiving to the ancestors. In short, *adat* can influence all aspects of life: economic, political, moral, spiritual, and social. It is seen by many as the social 'glue' that is necessary for communities to live peacefully together.

The attitude of the State towards *adat* has been ambiguous. The Dutch recognised the importance of local systems of authority; they codified much *adat* law and used it to reinforce governance at the local level. Although this sometimes resulted in rather grotesque distortions in order to serve the colonists' interests, it did for the most part allow for a continuation of local customs. But under the 1979 Village Government Act, village leaders had to be elected from a list of candidates approved by government officials. The criteria for candidacy included a minimum level of education and literacy, which excluded many *adat* leaders. The Act has been blamed for the destruction of traditional cultural and political systems in many areas. Coinciding with rapid urbanisation, which also tends to reduce the influence of traditional authority, this is widely believed to have contributed to much of the conflict and unrest that has plagued Indonesian society in recent years.

At a Butonese ceremony, held to mark the first time a child's feet touch the ground, an old woman spins the baby slowly around under a rack which holds parcels of cooked rice. He is then laid on a large banana leaf and smeared with oil. A big party follows, attended by all the family's friends and relatives. The baby's mother admits that she doesn't quite understand what's going on: 'I'm from Jakarta — we've come home to my husband's village for the ceremony — it's all new to me!'

A revival of *adat*?

The regional autonomy legislation of 1999 gives greater freedom to villages to organise their own leadership structures. It is believed that this could stimulate a revival and reform of *adat* traditions, and there are mixed feelings about the likely effect. Some feel that this shift could actually reduce people's opportunity to influence the governance of their community. Traditional societies are often strictly hierarchical, with rigid class or caste systems or gender roles determining people's position in the community, and making it difficult for a low-ranked person or a woman to fill a position of authority or be heard in public forums. The other concern is that an increased interest in *adat* will exclude newcomers who were not born into a particular society, and that this will lead to an increase in inter-ethnic tension.

On the other side, supporters of *adat* claim that its revival would reintroduce a sense of community into a society badly bruised by decades of intrusive State intervention. *Adat* codes could provide a much-needed alternative moral framework for a population disillusioned by *Pancasila*, and deeply mistrustful of their political leaders. Enthusiasts for *adat* argue that there is no reason why a revised form of traditional leadership cannot be used to build a new model for life in the twenty-first century.

An example of the potential of *adat* to rebuild communities is found in the Kei islands in Maluku. Here, traditional leaders were able to halt the escalation of inter-religious violence that swept across many islands in central and northern Maluku in 1999, and bring a swift end to the unrest.

▼ *Church and mosque stand side by side in the Kei Islands, Maluku. In Kei, traditional leaders were successful in resolving conflict between Christians and Muslims.*

Antonius Silubun, one of the *adat* leaders from Kei Besar, explained that when violence broke out between Christians and Muslims, he and the other elders travelled around to all the villages and hamlets on the island, reminding people that community tradition was more important than religious affiliations. After that, although violence still raged elsewhere, Kei Besar was peaceful. '*We protected each other*', Pak Antonius explains. '*Christian villagers sheltered Muslim neighbours whose houses had been destroyed. Even though people who had lost loved ones were angry and upset, they still listened to us.*' Local government officials were powerless to intervene, as nobody trusted them. '*The people here have nothing at all. We don't live in grand houses, but we do know about* adat.'

Language and literature

More than 600 languages and dialects are spoken in Indonesia, some by many millions of people (for example Javanese and Balinese), others by only a handful of older people in an isolated village. The majority have never existed in written form (only eight have an indigenous written literature), and many have not been fully documented. The official national language is Bahasa Indonesia, a version of the Malay spoken in the Malay peninsula and the western part of the island of Sumatra. A form of coastal Malay had been in wide use as a *lingua franca* along coastal shipping routes for centuries. The development of a national language was a powerful element in the independence struggle. While the Dutch colonial authorities had been reluctant to educate many Indonesians in Dutch, for fear of insubordination, the nationalists knew that an independent State would need a common vernacular means of communication. Most people speak a local language as their mother tongue, and in many rural areas it is not unusual to find people who do not speak Indonesian with confidence.

The development of Indonesian as a literary language was, in the first half of the twentieth century, closely related to the growing nationalist awareness among thinkers and writers in Java and Sumatra. Pramoedya Ananta Toer is one of Indonesia's best-known writers. His Buru Tetralogy, written while he was imprisoned on Buru island in Maluku under the New Order, traces both the development of nationalist feeling in the Dutch East Indies and the growing sophistication and subtlety of Bahasa Indonesia itself. Banned in Indonesia for many years, his writing is now being reissued and revalued. Other notable chroniclers of the independence struggle and the early years of the new nation include Mochtar Lubis, whose *Twilight in Jakarta* was first published in 1963.

The language today

With the increasing censorship and oppression of the New Order regime, the 1970s and 1980s was a rather barren period for Indonesian literature. Now that censorship laws have been lifted, there is a new vitality in the country's literature and journalism. Several hundred new media licences have been granted since 1999, and many new magazines and journals have appeared.

It is impossible to spend any time in Indonesia without becoming familiar with some of the numberless abbreviations used in daily speech and writing. Some are straightforward acronyms: KKN is *Korupsi, Kolusi dan Nepotisme*, the slogan of the reformation movement; TNI is *Tentara Nasional Indonesia*, the Indonesian Army. Others are far more inventive and need some disentangling. DepDikNas, for example, is *Departemen Pendidikan Nasional*, the Department of Education, and a *balita* is an *anak bawah lima tahun* (a child under five years old). Acronyms can cause considerable confusion, because the same letters may refer to several different things. There is also fun to be had: KKN may refer to a serious political critique, but it is also *kuliah kerja nyata*, the practical community service which university students have to complete before graduation; this phrase in turn is adapted to *kawin kemudian nikah*, or 'sex before marriage', as a wry comment on what student community service often involves!

▲ *A huge dragon statue at the Chinese temple, Surabaya. In 2002 it was the scene of the first full-scale celebrations of the Chinese New Year to be permitted for a generation.*

Chinese Indonesians: privilege and prejudice

Tuesday 12 February 2002, early evening, Chinese Temple, Surabaya: around 5000 people are gathered excitedly together. The occasion? Imlek – Chinese New Year 4699, the Year of the Horse. Inside, the temple shimmers with gold-leaf decoration. People bring offerings of fruit and stand in front of altars, holding great bunches of incense sticks above their heads with both hands. A huge pile of discarded incense lies smoking outside; the air is thick with it and swelters in the heat of hundreds of candles. Outside, a gigantic sculpture depicting two rearing dragons, mouths wide open, surrounded by Chinese figures, frames the evening sky. Chubby Chinese children run around as preparations are concluded, and people take their seats in front of a stage for the celebrations. A fairly standard picture of cultural commemoration, you might imagine – an annual event.

Not so. This is the first time Chinese New Year has been celebrated on this scale in Indonesia since repressive legislation restricted Chinese cultural and economic activities in the late 1950s. Anti-Chinese feeling in Indonesia is rooted in economic interests and rivalries, and is particularly acute during periods of political and economic upheaval. Despite their economic success, Chinese Indonesians still occupy a precarious position within Indonesian society.

Instruments of the government: a double-edged sword

Traders have been visiting Indonesia from China for more than a thousand years, but there were surges of migration in the seventeenth and nineteenth centuries. During the colonial period, the Dutch welcomed Chinese immigrants and allowed them to form a commercial middle class between native Indonesians and the colonial elite. From the earliest times, Chinese people were set apart from the rest of the population, often compelled to live in designated areas, or wear certain clothes to identify them. Chinese people were not allowed to own land, so they turned to trade, with considerable success. Although Chinese people were often used to mediate between the native population and the colonial authorities, they did not acquire any significant political power, and soon became the target of local resentment, acting as scapegoats during periods of economic hardship.

In 1959, amid growing social unrest, Sukarno passed a series of restrictions on citizenship for Chinese Indonesians, who were banned from owning businesses in rural areas. Less than a decade later, the Suharto government passed Presidential Decree No. 14/1967, extending the trading restrictions to include involvement in transport, food, and banking, and imposing heavy additional taxation on ethnic Chinese traders. This law banned all public cultural activities and religious practices, and prohibited the use of Chinese language and script in any medium, apart from one approved newspaper. The numbers of Chinese who could enter the civil service, the universities, and the military were limited. Chinese Indonesians had to carry specially marked identity cards, and were encouraged to take Indonesian names.

Ethnic Chinese today, numbering about seven million, constitute only three per cent of the Indonesian population, but are thought to control between 70 and 80 per cent of non-land, private corporate wealth. Aside from a few fabulously wealthy families, however, most of them are small traders and shopkeepers. During the New Order, the notorious term *cukong* (financier) described the close relationship between Chinese men and women in business and the government officials who took advantage of the Chinese minority status to profit from providing protection and influence. By the 1980s the Suharto family's fortunes had become closely intertwined with the continuing success of the Chinese. The Chinese tycoons remained dependent on the military to protect them from the rancour of the general population. As long as the economy remained healthy, however, their position was safe.

This state of affairs was not to last. As the economic crisis gripped the nation in early 1998, the government revealed that Chinese people owned nine of the top ten business groups in the country, and that 13 of the top 15 taxpayers were Chinese. Anti-Chinese feeling erupted across the country, as prices of basic goods rose sharply. Chinese shopkeepers who raised their prices accordingly were seen as profiting from the crisis, and Chinese businesses and shops were attacked and burned in many areas.

Desheng Wang is 50 years old and has lived in Surabaya all his life. His family has lived in Indonesia for three generations. Although some of his relatives have married Javanese people, he can't forget the Chinese blood in his veins, and calls himself a Chinese Indonesian – '*I still have yellow skin!*' Desheng Wang is cautiously optimistic about the future. '*Things will take two generations to work out. Democracy is as yet only a thin veneer – only skin-deep.*' He feels that the Chinese community is still not allowed to speak freely (and he didn't want to be photographed). '*It's great that we are not now limited to only one officially sanctioned newspaper, for example. But all this can be taken away, even the freedom to practise our traditional ceremonies.*'

In May 1998, as the general economic and political crisis deepened, the Chinese community was the target of violent attacks during riots in Jakarta. More than 1000 people were killed in two days of carnage, many in burning shopping malls. Human-rights groups allege that nearly 170 Chinese women were systematically targeted for rape, of whom about 20 subsequently died. It is widely rumoured that the violence was condoned, if not organised, by the authorities, keen to find a scapegoat to deflect attention from the government's own failings. After the riots, many Chinese Indonesians took their money out of the country, and not all have returned.

A cautious new start

President Wahid revoked the 1967 Decree in 2000, and Imlek has now been declared an optional holiday. In 2002, many of the Chinese-owned factories in Surabaya, a city with a large Chinese population, were closed throughout the holiday period, and even the President took the day off. There are calls to give Imlek the same status as other religious holidays. Mandarin schools are springing up all over the city, and the Chinese-language press has blossomed. But many other discriminatory laws have not yet been reviewed, and the momentum of reform seems to have slowed down. Even slower to change are generations of ingrained prejudice towards the ethnic Chinese community.

It remains to be seen whether the spirit of *reformasi* has the ability or the will to extend to a permanent change in the position of Chinese Indonesians.

▼ *Prayers to mark the New Year at the Chinese temple, Surabaya. Many ethnic Chinese welcome the recent relaxation of restrictions on their community, but remain fearful that the new-found freedom could be revoked.*

Agriculture: back to the future?

With a huge population to sustain, and increasing numbers living in urban areas, the state of agriculture in Indonesia is extremely important. More than half of Indonesians are farmers, mostly on small, family-owned plots of land; very often women perform many of the central agricultural tasks. In Java and Sumatra, and parts of Sulawesi and Nusa Tenggara, as well as all urban areas, rice is the staple food, and paddy fields occupy a large proportion of agricultural land. In other areas, particularly those with poor or drier soils, maize or tubers such as cassava and sweet potato are the main subsistence crops. Several varieties of vegetable are grown widely, as are a huge range of fruit trees, providing mangoes, papaya, durian, citrus fruits, jackfruit, and bananas, among many others. Farmers also produce several cash crops for export, including copra, cocoa, tea, and coffee.

Recent years have brought particular problems for farmers in Indonesia. A succession of droughts and floods has upset planting and harvest patterns, and reduced yields. The effects of the economic crisis, while less severe for most farmers than for urban workers, have put pressure on reserves and a strain on resources. Farmers have responded to these challenges in a range of ways, reflecting their ability to combine traditional wisdom with modern thinking to best effect.

▼ *Rice is the staple food of many Indonesians, and women play a central role in its cultivation.*

Rice production and the Green Revolution

In the years following independence, Indonesia's rice production failed to keep pace with population growth, which led to a large deficit by the early 1970s. Indonesia was the world's largest importer of rice by 1980. Seeing that rapid industrialisation would only lead to more urban mouths for farmers to feed, the New Order

▲ *Pounding rice in a Sumba village. For a brief period in the 1980s, Indonesia was self-sufficient in rice.*

government began a drive to self-sufficiency by expanding the area of agricultural land available for rice cultivation, at the same time as using the new technologies of the so-called Green Revolution to intensify production.

The policy was successful – but at a very heavy price. Rice production increased threefold under the New Order; in 1984 Indonesia achieved self-sufficiency, and was even able to provide food aid to Africa. By the mid-1990s, however, the less desirable effects of this policy were clearly apparent. Intensification demanded new high-yielding rice varieties, a uniform planting and harvesting schedule, and artificial fertilisers and pesticides in large quantities. To encourage farmers to adopt the new methods, and to stimulate domestic industry, the government subsidised the cost of pesticides and fertilisers by up to 82 per cent until the mid-1980s. The *rumus tani,* or 'farmer's formula', explicitly linked the price of rice with the cost of fertilisers. Use of chemical inputs shot up, as did the government's subsidy bill.

The hidden costs of modernisation

Not only were the costs to the government considerable, but farmers found that increased use of chemicals gradually destroyed local eco-systems, leading to a growing dependency on chemical pesticides and fertilisers. There has been an increase in pesticide-resistance, and a reduction of natural predators. Run-off water from irrigated land full of pesticides has polluted rivers, damaging fish stocks and contaminating supplies of drinking water. Now that the subsidies have been withdrawn, and production has been handed over to private businesses, fertilisers and pesticides have become more expensive. Not only that, but it is now more difficult for the government to regulate the use of toxic chemicals, and many farmers have suffered ill-health through their use.

Indonesian farmers traditionally combine rice-growing with raising fish and ducks, and growing fruit and vegetables. This combination helps to maintain a stable eco-system which is an effective form of pest control, as well as providing a variety of food for the family. But self-sufficiency in rice demanded a continuous cycle, yielding two or even three crops per year. This meant that the traditional planting of legumes and vegetables after the rice harvest was discontinued in many places, and the planting of fruit trees alongside rice paddies also declined. Local rice varieties were rejected in favour of Green Revolution hybrids, the seed for which cannot

▲ *A farmer herds his ducks along a road in Java. Ducks thrive in the wet environment of the paddy fields and provide an additional source of food and income for farming families.*

be saved: it has to be bought fresh each time. Along with the additional expense, this led to the loss of collective systems for saving seed in rice banks for the next planting, and for insurance against a failed harvest. Perhaps most significantly, the rigid, top–down system permitted no local decision-making or analysis of environmental conditions, and made no allowance for the role of farming in cultural and religious traditions. In Bali, for example, irrigation systems and the agricultural cycle are traditionally determined by priests of the water temples, not by government directive. In many areas, women's traditional roles in the cycle of planting and harvest have been diminished. The result has been a loss of local farming expertise, a feeling of powerlessness among farmers, and a decline in community feeling as collective traditions are weakened in the struggle to meet ever-higher production targets.

Since the mid-1990s, national rice production has been in decline. Prices for external inputs such as fertiliser, driven up by the economic crisis, and increased competition from cheap imported rice have made rice production less and less viable for many farmers. The main beneficiaries of government policies of price control and fertiliser subsidy were the 20 per cent of farmers who own more than half a hectare of wet rice paddy and could use the new technology to its full advantage. Many small farmers have fallen into debt and subsequently lost their land through having to take out large loans to pay for inputs. Others, especially on crowded Java, have sold their land to developers; between 40,000 and 50,000 hectares of rice fields are converted for non-agricultural purposes every year on Java alone, which produces sixty per cent of the national crop.

Much of the reduction, however, is a planned response by farmers to the threat of drought. Rice is more dependent on sufficient water supplies than any other staple crop, so when *El Niño* delayed the rains at the end of 1997, many farmers had already insured themselves against total harvest failure by planting maize, soybeans, and tubers alongside (or instead of) rice. Since the end of the New Order, farmers have once again begun to make their own decisions about how to farm their land. The result in some areas has been an increasing diversity of crops, a diminishing reliance on chemical inputs, and a renewed sense of pride and ownership among farming communities.

Alternatives to the Green Revolution: organic farming in Java

At first glance, Pak Sukahar's farm looks much like any other in central Java. There is rice paddy, a vegetable plot, and a cow in a stall. Look closer, however, and a couple of things stand out. A thick hedge divides his plot from neighbouring land, and the end of every row of vegetables is planted with red flowers. Pak Sukahar's farm is organic. The hedge protects his crops from the chemicals used on other farms nearby, and the red flowers attract pests away from the vegetables.

Javanese farmers are finding that their land, requiring more and more chemicals to maintain yields, is gradually becoming infertile. It's not surprising, therefore, that some have decided to try to break the cycle of increased chemical use by making their farms organic. It's a slow and labour-intensive process, but there is a growing market for organic produce, and it means that small farmers are less dependent on expensive external inputs.

Although Pak Sukahar began the organic conversion of his land in 1991, it took five years to clear it of chemicals and to develop suitable seed, returning to traditional local varieties which can be saved from season to season. As well as rice, Pak Sukahar grows a wide variety of fruit and vegetables, including chillies, onions, strawberries, and lettuce. The more varieties you plant, he explains, the less danger there is of everything being destroyed by pests. Strawberries are the current bestseller. Pak Sukahar's plot yields about 4kg every three days,

▼ *Pak Sukahar with his crop of organic strawberries*

which he can sell to supermarkets for Rp25,000 a kilo (about £2.00). The return on rice is not so great: a kilo of organic rice sells for only Rp500 more than conventional rice, but as he sells through a co-operative he gets a stable price for the whole season, and is protected from fluctuations in the market.

Pak Sukahar makes his own organic fertilisers and pesticides, using animal dung, compost, and micro-organisms. He even sells some of his fertiliser, but says that, although he could easily monopolise the local market, he prefers to teach others how to make it. '*Conventional farmers only think about their sales income, and don't consider how much they spend on chemicals. It's one of the reasons why I went organic*', he says.

The real farming experts

Pak Mahdjo has a rice farm in the village of Seyegan, near Yogyakarta. He and other local farmers have been experimenting with organic methods since 1991. The New Order government was very suspicious of anyone who did not follow the government programmes, and the farmers were kept under strict surveillance by local officials. '*We had to be brave!*', he says. Since *reformasi* they are not harassed by the authorities any longer, but still it is hard to persuade people to change their farming habits. Many of the young farmers nowadays have grown up with New Order policies and know nothing of traditional farming methods. The economic crisis has encouraged increasing numbers of people to become more

▼ *West Sumba: ploughing rice fields with buffalo is often more effective and efficient than using machinery.*

Demand for organic produce is slowly growing, as wealthier consumers seek out healthier, tastier, chemical-free food. But public awareness of the meaning of 'organic agriculture' remains very low in Indonesia. More and more traders are claiming that their products are organic, but there is no way of knowing where this rice actually comes from. As yet there is no national certification or labelling scheme. The government hopes to make Indonesia one of the largest organic producers by 2010, and has established a Commission to certify organic products; but there is concern that this could discriminate against small farmers, if they have to meet stringent processing requirements which only larger businesses can sustain. Farmers' groups in central Java are working with NGOs, consumers, and academics to develop an organic 'mark', based on agreed standards, which will inform and protect the consumer, at the same time as respecting the identity of individual farmers and supporting a more community-based approach to farming.

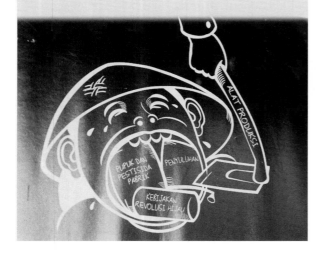

▲ A cartoon critical of the government's Green Revolution agricultural policy, which coerced farmers to use chemical fertilisers

self-sufficient through organic methods, to save money on chemical inputs. The farmers form groups of around 35 people to improve the efficiency of their small plots. This way they can share the costs and labour involved in ploughing with buffalo: '*It's a much better method than using a tractor, as all those feet mean that the soil is ploughed deeper, and buffalo don't require any expensive spare parts!*'

Pak Mahdjo has been in demand recently by university researchers keen to learn the secrets of his success. '*We just learned about making fertiliser through trial and error,*' he laughs, '*but the scientists want to know how many grammes of everything we use!*' He says their organic rice tastes sweeter, keeps better, and feeds more people per kilo. It is good-quality food, which does not require much cash outlay: '*Why grow organic rice and eat instant noodles?*'

Farming Sumba-style

The island of Sumba lies at the eastern end of the Nusa Tenggara chain, which begins in Bali and ends in Timor. Although it is relatively small – only 210 km from end to end – both the landscape and the culture are distinctive. The drier eastern part is mountainous, with high grassy plateaux and deep, forested river valleys. The west is wetter and more densely populated. Sumba is known for its beautiful woven *ikat* cloths, and for the visually spectacular nature of its traditions. Huge megalithic stone tombs punctuate the landscape between the traditional bamboo houses, built on stilts with high-peaked, grass-thatched roofs. The annual *Pasola* festival draws huge crowds. Sumba is a good example of a rural Indonesian community struggling to make a living, often under difficult circumstances, and trying to combine traditional and modern influences to best effect.

Thirty or forty years ago the staple foods on Sumba, as in many areas in eastern Indonesia, were maize, cassava, some dry-rice varieties, and various other types of tuber. Nowadays, much of this area is planted with wet rice. Using Green Revolution rhetoric, the New Order government persuaded many eastern Indonesian communities that it was more civilised to eat non-indigenous rice varieties, and that those who relied on

► *During* Pasola, *an annual Sumbanese festival, mounted 'warriors' charge at each other, armed with spears. Although the government tries to fix the date in advance, in order to attract tourists, traditional priests have the final say.*

traditional crops were less advanced. In effect, the goal of rice self-sufficiency came to mean persuading everyone to grow and eat rice, regardless of whether it was appropriate for local conditions.

The result was a neglect of root crops in preference for rice; but, with the restrictions of technology and the environment, Sumbanese farmers can supply themselves with rice for a maximum of only five months of the year. Sumba is now heavily dependent on rice imports, especially from nearby Flores, which of course must be paid for. One kilo of rice costs as much as two kilos of maize or cassava, which leaves little spare cash for sources of protein and vitamins. As a result, there are regular hungry months in many Sumbanese households. A brief period between harvests has always existed, when traditionally people would go foraging in the forest to supplement their food stocks – the Sumbanese call it *mandara*. Nowadays this is less and less of an option, as access to forests is restricted and the pressure on resources becomes greater. Regular food shortages are becoming more of a problem, forcing many people into debt to feed their families. This shift from subsistence agriculture to a system which requires cash for the purchase of basic foodstuffs has occurred in many parts of rural Indonesia.

A plague of locusts

Another threat to Sumbanese livelihoods is the locust. Community workers say that the infestations appear to occur in 15-year cycles, devastating all kinds of crops, and ruining seed stocks for the following year. The unusually dry weather in recent years has compounded the problem. Locals suggest a different explanation for the plagues. They say that the locusts were sent by the gods to purge the land and restore harmony after it was poisoned by over-use of chemicals. Proof of this,

▲ *A woman from a farmers' collective in East Sumba demonstrates damage to crops caused by locusts.*

they explain, is in the fact that, after government officials attempted to kill the locusts with yet more chemical sprays, their vehicle slipped on the bodies of the insects and skidded off the road. Not long after that, fields owned by one of the officials were attacked by the locusts and completely destroyed.

Group therapy

Whatever the cause, the effects are clear. A combination of ill-advised government policy and serious pest problems has left Sumbanese agriculture in a precarious state. However, local people have developed a series of measures to try to protect themselves from these uncertainties. Traditionally, planting and harvest activities are done co-operatively, with informal working groups pitching in to help to work everybody's land – a common practice all over the archipelago. More recently, with the help of local NGOs, many farmers have organised themselves into more permanent farming groups, running small-scale savings and credit schemes and rotating livestock-breeding programmes, and establishing *lumbung paceklik*, or 'famine rice barns', to save seed for planting in the following year, or for emergencies when harvests fail.

Although the weather, the locusts, and other pests have recently strained these resources to the limit, and many people have had to sell livestock to meet needs for food and education, the groups are still going strong. The social as well as economic benefits of such groups are clear. Many of the groups are run by and for women, offering members the chance to meet regularly away from home, and a valuable opportunity to share concerns and ask advice about a wide range of issues, including health and child care. The groups have also been the focus for classes in Indonesian language and basic literacy and numeracy, designed to help local people to understand and defend their rights. One woman explained that now they know if they are being cheated by traders, and they can understand what is going on at government meetings. Other training sessions, run by the local NGOs, include courses on gender awareness. One woman says, *'Before, it was only the teachers who knew things. Now that we get invited to all kinds of things, even if we don't become experts, we at least learn something.'*

CULTURE AND AGRICULTURE: TWO PARTS OF A WHOLE

High in the hills above the town of Waitabula, in western Sumba, the village of Totok perches on a steep ridge, commanding breathtaking views towards the sea. This is not rice-growing country: the land is steep and stony, and there is a chronic shortage of water. Local farmers grow maize and cassava, and are experimenting with onions and fruit trees. Times are hard: the last onion harvest failed because of bad weather, and villagers' crops have been affected by pests. Their explanation for this run of misfortune is straightforward. The village's sacred ceremonial house, centre of cultural and ritual life, is in a poor state. The original one, with a roof soaring seven metres high, burned down many years ago. Its replacement, with a roof of only four metres, has never been satisfactory and needs rebuilding, but there is no money to do this: the correct procedure requires not only construction materials but also substantial animal sacrifices. Although they are nominally Christian ('*If the government asks, we're Catholics,*' says one traditional elder, '*but actually we have two religions, and ceremonies for both*'), people's lives in Totok are organised around traditional beliefs and practices. The annual calendar is marked by a cycle of rituals which trace the pattern of the agricultural year, combining thanksgiving for harvests with rain-making ceremonies. Tradition remains a most powerful force in village life, influencing everything from morality to war (conflict with neighbouring villages is not uncommon), and is a source of great pride and community cohesion. But Totok people are also keen to participate in the wider world, and are putting traditional expertise to economic use by selling home-forged knives in local markets: '*Just because we are far from the city doesn't mean we don't have skills*'.

◄ *Queuing for water in Totok village*

Empowering women

Although most men on Sumba now seem to support their wives' activities, this was not always the case. There was an increase in levels of domestic violence when the women's groups were established, as some husbands resented the time that their wives spent out of the house, apparently neglecting their household duties. The solution has been to involve families as a whole in the groups. One woman, who is a group co-ordinator, explains how she feels far more confident now about speaking up in public, and that the experience has had a positive impact on women's representation in other areas of village life. *'Before, if someone spoke to me in Indonesian,*

▲ *A women's savings and credit group, Waingapu, East Sumba. Group meetings give members a valued opportunity to discuss child care and health matters with other women.*

I would be afraid to reply. Now, when the men meet in the traditional assembly to discuss issues relating to weddings and dowries, the women have their say as well. Before, we just used to be in the kitchen, and our voices were never heard.' The division of labour in the household has also become more equal, with men sharing more of the domestic chores, such as cooking and collecting water.

Young people are encouraged to contribute the skills that they learn at school, by keeping the groups' accounts and managing the administration. It is one way of persuading young people to consider staying in their communities. As in many rural areas of Indonesia, there is a tendency for educated young people to aspire to civil-service positions: an office job, however poorly valued and low-paid, is seen as more prestigious than working the land. Very often this ambition leads the most talented young people to leave rural areas.

It is too early to say whether initiatives such as the farmers' groups will alter this trend. Other problems, such as the stranglehold of local middlemen over produce markets, have yet to be resolved. Some farmers are excluded from joining groups because they live too far away. But the Sumbanese farmers are full of enthusiasm and ideas for the future. One group are planning to experiment with new cash crops such as coffee and vanilla alongside subsistence agriculture, and hope that the local NGO will help them to use traditional pest-control methods more effectively. According to one group member, *'The farmers' group means we can begin to think ahead a little, rather than simply living from day to day.'*

The struggle for land and resources

February 2002 saw some of the worst-ever floods in central Jakarta. While serious flooding is a regular problem in many areas, the chaos caused in the capital city made the issue impossible to ignore. Five-star hotels and even the President's palace were awash, the road to the airport was impassable, and people had to be rescued from their houses in boats after water levels rose to a peak of eight metres in some parts of the city. Thirty people lost their lives, and hundreds of thousands of people were forced to flee from their homes.

It was quickly recognised that this was no natural disaster. 'Jakarta is paying for its sins', said people in other areas. Whether or not one can attach a moral significance to the floods, it is clear that a corrupt political and administrative system has not helped matters. Collusion between government officials and large real-estate developers weakened the implementation of planning regulations and permitted widespread deforestation on the steep slopes around Jakarta. The rainwater poured off the hillsides, with nothing to impede its advance.

The story is not unique to Jakarta – far from it. Decades of State-sponsored exploitation of Indonesia's natural resources, with little regard for environmental consequences, have made communities all over the country increasingly vulnerable to the effects of droughts and floods, forest fires, and landslides. The government's failure to recognise traditional land rights has weakened local people's sense of connection to the land on which they rely. The involvement of multinational corporations in exploiting natural resources has further disempowered local people. Nevertheless, some communities are trying to regain control of their environment and protect themselves and their livelihoods from disasters, whether natural or man-made.

▼ *Jakarta, February 2002: residents wade through the water in the capital city's worst-ever recorded floods*

The morning of 22 November 1994 began much as any other in the hamlet of Turgo, on the slopes of Mount Merapi near Yogyakarta in central Java. Farmers left their homes in the early morning to work their fields and tend their animals. One family was preparing for a wedding party. Mount Merapi, one of the world's most active volcanoes, had been showing signs of increased activity for several months, but that morning nothing seemed out of the ordinary. Around ten o'clock the wedding guests began to arrive. An hour later a pyroclastic surge swept down the mountain without warning and engulfed the whole area. Forty-three villagers died.

There are definite advantages to living on the slopes of a volcano. Eruptions in 1954 and 1961 left a thick covering of ash, which makes the soil extremely fertile. Land is more plentiful on the mountain than on the more crowded plains below. However, the pyroclastic surge took everyone by surprise. The official early-warning system, which is rather bureaucratic, failed to alert the villagers in time.

The 1994 eruption destroyed Mahjo Utomo's house, and left him with severe injuries. *'It all happened very fast'*, he explains. *'I put my cows in their pen and then it went dark, and the* awan panas [literally 'hot cloud'] *came down from the volcano.'* After the disaster the government decided that Turgo was unsafe. It offered the inhabitants the choice of relocation to a nearby safe area, or transmigration far away from the region. Many people felt that the psychological trauma of forced relocation was greater than the physical and financial suffering caused by the eruption. *'The government is only concerned about our physical safety'*, they complained. *'It doesn't care how we feel.'* Although many villagers moved back to Turgo illegally, until 1999 the government refused to recognise the hamlet, excluding its inhabitants from the provision of basic services.

Early warning Turgo-style

After the 1994 eruption, people in Turgo decided to take responsibility for their own safety. Pak Mahjo rebuilt his house with a concrete bunker, complete with ventilation holes, to protect him and his family from future eruptions. People began to re-apply traditional knowledge, learning how to read the signs of the mountain from their own experience, rather than relying on scientific instruments. The villagers have built their own observation post and reinstated a system of alarms which is activated by hitting bamboo gongs hung outside each house. In an area with no electricity, and only one or two radios, this is an effective way of spreading information quickly. People also pay close attention to the movements of wild animals and birds. A false alarm in 2000 was a good test of the new system. When the authorities arrived to evacuate the village, they found it deserted: the people of Turgo had successfully organised their own evacuation. Pak Mahjo says, *'The early-warning programme enables villagers to work together as a community to protect their futures.'*

FOREST FIRES

The forest fires that raged across Indonesia in 1997/98 in the wake of *El Niño* made headline news all over the world. A huge pall of haze hung across South-East Asia as the fires burned out of control. It is estimated that more than five million hectares of forest were destroyed in East Kalimantan alone, at a cost of around US$ 9 billion. Some 75 million people were affected by the fires, smoke, and haze.

Forest fires are not a new phenomenon: serious fires followed droughts in 1982, 1987, 1991, and 1994. But the dramatic scale of the 1997/98 fires drew attention to the role of Indonesia's land-management policy in compounding the effects of a natural hazard. Most of the area that burned consisted of timber concessions, plantations, and fallow agricultural land, especially those areas that had been recently logged. The Indonesian government has always blamed slash-and-burn agriculturalists for causing the fires; it claimed that 85 per cent of the 1994 fires were started by local farmers. After the 1997/98 outbreak, however, it was forced to recognise the role of logging and plantation companies. While it is true that some farmers do use fire to clear agricultural land, plantation owners do this on a far larger scale, and with fewer concerns about the potential risks of such action during a drought.

The 1999 Forestry Act makes provision for the prosecution of companies who have forest fires on their land, regardless of who actually struck the match. What is lacking, however, is the political will to implement the legislation. Logging concessions and plantations were one of the mainstays of economic development during the New Order, part of a far-reaching network of 'crony capitalism', involving politicians and the military as well as big business. Eighty per cent of the 1997/98 fires occurred on land owned by companies connected to the Suharto family and their friends. Successful prosecutions are rare, and hundreds of cases are pending. Meanwhile, the threat of serious forest fires has become an annual phenomenon.

▶ *The temporary home of a miner near a sand quarry on the slopes of Mount Merapi. The quarrying began as an effort to excavate channels down the mountain to deflect volcanic lava away from villages, but the extraction business proved so profitable that dozens of trucks a day trundle up and down the slopes, creating massive problems of erosion.*

Disappearing forests

Indonesia contains ten per cent of the world's remaining tropical forests. It also has one of the highest deforestation rates in the world: 1.7 million hectares are lost every year. The World Resources Institute estimates that Indonesia will lose 12.5 per cent of its forest cover in the next ten years; the World Bank predicts that lowland forests could be extinct in Sumatra by 2005, and in Kalimantan not long after 2010. It is estimated that up to 70 per cent of timber from Indonesia is logged illegally. Eighty per cent of the habitat of Indonesia's orang utans has disappeared over the last 20 years, and some suggest that this species could disappear from the wild within a decade.

▲ *Putussibau, West Kalimantan: a Dayak man enters the rainforest carrying a chainsaw. Abandoning their traditional role of 'forest keepers', some Dayaks are tempted to take cash from illegal logging companies, in return for cutting trees for them.*

These are alarming statistics, but they do not tell us who is destroying Indonesia's forests, or why. These are critical questions: many of Indonesia's problems stem from conflicts over unequal access to land and natural resources, and uneven distribution of the revenue from the exploitation of resources. The key to understanding the fate of the forests is the relationships between the government and local communities, plantation owners, and logging companies. The combined power of big business and a government intent on reducing its burden of foreign debt remains a serious threat to Indonesia's forests.

Protecting rural livelihoods in Java

Although most forest land in Indonesia is in Sumatra, West Papua, and Kalimantan, some of the fiercest battles over control of forest resources occur in far more densely populated areas, where the pressure on land is at its greatest, and the effects of its degradation are most harmful. In many cases, those who suffer most are the poorest people, who cannot move their livelihoods elsewhere.

Much forest land in Java is worked as monoculture plantations of teak or mahogany. Monocultures mature uniformly, and the trees are all clear-felled at the same time, leaving bare land which is prone to erosion. Very often these plantations are on land customarily owned by a village, although villagers' use of it is severely restricted. They are allowed to grow crops between the seedling trees in the first two or three years of a plantation's life, before the trees grow too tall. After that, they have no access to the land at all, and cannot hunt wild animals or collect non-timber forest products, although the plantation owners themselves have no interest in harvesting them. In an area as densely populated as Java, this can cause severe pressure on agricultural land. Typically, only 20 per cent of a village's customary land can be used for rice cultivation, because of competition from a plantation. With these kinds of restriction, many villages struggle to produce enough food for subsistence. The fight for the land in these areas is in deadly earnest: desperate villagers resort to illegal logging to survive, while concession-holders protect their plantations with armed guards.

Government supervision of plantations and timber concessions is very limited, partly owing to logistical difficulties and lack of resources, partly through indifference. Some local groups in east Java are therefore taking it upon themselves to supervise the activities of both legitimate and illegal loggers, and to report them to the authorities; a local NGO, the Centre for Environmental Education (*Pusat Pendidikan Lingkungan Hidup* – PPLH), acts as mediator. With the support of PPLH, some farmers have also begun a limited reforestation project, replanting 15 hectares of mixed forest in a degraded watershed area, with plans for more.

Prayer for the forest

Arief Ramanato, from PPLH, is encouraged by this: '*After so many years of repression, people feel little sense of belonging towards their land, and need plenty of support to defend it. The government encourages people to be modern, but they risk losing important traditional knowledge. These villagers are just beginning to value again the wisdom of their ancestors in protecting watersheds and replanting trees.*' In support of this, PPLH organised an event called 'Prayer for the Forest', gathering together local villagers, environmentalists, artists, NGOs, students, government officials, and businessmen for a programme of seminars and performances, as an expression of concern for the fate of the forests, and a celebration of traditional culture.

Although such local initiatives are a sign of positive change, Indonesia's forests remain in the middle of a tug of war between local and central government. Under the new decentralisation legislation, Jakarta is encouraging regions to become economically viable, suggesting that autonomy could be rescinded if profitability is not achieved. There is a danger that, with this pressure, and with new control over the management of natural resources, regional governments could treat forests as a source of revenue rather than as a sustainable resource which they have a responsibility to manage for the benefit of the community.

The fishing industry: sharing the sea

With more than three million square kilometres of sea, and some of the most plentiful fishing grounds in the world, it is hardly surprising that the fishing industry is so important to Indonesia. This bounty is evident in any coastal town or village. Fish markets offer a fantastic array of seafood for sale:

huge shiny silver tuna nestle next to barracuda, squid, crabs, and plump juicy prawns. There are some less familiar sights too: the insignificant-looking *teripang*, or sea cucumber, is a delicacy highly prized by the Chinese, as are sharks' fins, used for medicine and for the famous soup. Some fish is dried and salted to preserve it for transportation, or to feed the family through seasons when the sea may be too rough for small boats to go to sea. While it is usually men who go out in boats to fish, in many communities women and children participate in gathering sea produce from the shoreline and shallow water, and women are often responsible for transporting the fish to market and selling it.

Enterprises range from the activities of a single fisherman with an outrigger canoe to the operations of huge transnational companies. All are important to the Indonesian economy, but large and small concerns do not always co-exist happily, and small fisherfolk are often forced out by foreign firms with larger boats. The legal status of Indonesian waters does not help matters, as it makes it difficult for local government to regulate and benefit from incomers. There are also concerns about dwindling fish stocks, even in areas traditionally considered under-exploited, and there are reports of destructive and unsustainable fishing methods.

Making a living from the sea

Sometimes the difference between working in poor conditions in order to survive and being in control of one's fate is simply the size of a boat. Fishermen in the village of Bone Bone in Buton, off the south-east coast

▼ *Kei Islands, Maluku: small fishermen often struggle to compete with the fleets of large boats owned by commercial companies.*

of Sulawesi, specialise in catching *cekalang*, a type of tuna which is destined for export. For the last ten years most fishermen in the village have been employed by people from Flores (an island south of Buton), who own larger boats. '*We're lucky in some ways*', says one fisherman, La Ode Mu'min. '*Before the Flores people came, we only used our* sampans [small outrigger sailing boats]*, and couldn't go very far out.*' But there are also disadvantages. The boat owners take an extortionate 50 per cent of the catch, and they manipulate prices at will, which can make them very unstable, but local fishermen are afraid to protest, for fear of being sacked. '*I'd never have stuck it for so long, but I have no choice.*'

The Buton fishermen want to raise the capital to buy their own boats, but it is difficult to obtain a loan without security. The other problem is their isolation. It isn't easy to buy good fibreglass boats and outboard motors in a remote area, and even more difficult to get hold of spare parts. '*People don't want to be bothered with the labour-intensive process of caulking the seams of a wooden boat with cotton soaked in coconut oil any more – but relying on modern technology has its own problems.*'

Some groups of small fisherfolk in the Kei Islands in Maluku make a living from catching live coral fish, such as the Napoleon Wrasse. These fish fetch a good price, but their fragile habitat needs to be carefully maintained in order to ensure a sustainable supply. One group became increasingly annoyed with a Hong Kong firm which owned a factory near their village. The company was using cyanide to poison the fish, and bombs to stun them. These methods are illegal, as they pollute the water and kill the coral. The local people repeatedly reported these activities to the authorities, but no action was taken. Fish stocks have declined noticeably over the last five years, and fishermen are becoming fearful for their livelihoods.

Alongside the small fishermen working from their outrigger canoes in Kei stands a gigantic fish-refrigeration plant, owned by the Suharto family. Several foreign ships are moored at the quayside. Large national and international conglomerates of this kind threaten the livelihoods of small fishermen in many areas of Indonesia. Without refrigeration facilities, or direct access to markets, small fishermen find it hard to compete with such large players.

Monitoring of fishing rights and activity, and allocation of revenue derived from fishing in Indonesian waters are hampered by a complicated system of boundaries, which divide responsibility between district, provincial, and national government. Local government officials in Kei say this system makes it difficult for them to regulate large foreign vessels, which are granted permits at provincial or national levels. Regional autonomy makes this discrepancy even more striking. While local government gets increasing control over the use of and revenue from local land, it has very little influence over marine matters: '*It's local land, but still national sea*', says one official.

Livelihoods away from the land

Although agriculture is extremely important to Indonesia's people and economy, not everyone makes a living from the land. Eighty million people live in Indonesia's cities, almost 11 million of them in Jakarta alone. For urban residents, and those running small businesses in rural areas, access to land and natural resources is less important than earning a living wage in adequate working conditions, and being able to compete equally in the market. The economic crisis has increased the pressure on non-agricultural livelihoods, leaving many people more vulnerable to exploitation and insecurity.

Children at work

Surabaya is Indonesia's second city, and its industrial heartland, with many of the country's largest plastics, clothing, and cigarette factories, and one of its busiest ports. Young people come from surrounding villages and small towns to work in Surabaya in order to supplement their families' income. Many of them are girls. Faced with the choice of which children to take out of education and put to work, families more often decide to educate their sons. Employers prefer girls, as they are believed to be more diligent and easier to control than boys. The children live in crowded rented accommodation and often work up to 12 hours a day.

Throughout Indonesia, it is common for families to encourage their children to begin to work at an early age. Three-quarters of working children work as unpaid labourers in a family business while they learn how to run it in the future. It's part of the experience of growing up. Half of working children also attend school. Since the crisis of the late 1990s, however, economic necessity has driven children into formal employment. Research has indicated a sharp increase in the numbers of under-age children trying to get factory work. Employment in factories, often away from the family, has particular dangers for young workers, and is difficult to combine with education.

On paper, Indonesia provides good legislative protection for child labourers. No one under the age of 15 is allowed to work in a factory, and officially those between 15 and 18 may not work more than eight hours a day. In practice, however, these regulations are poorly enforced.

Reliable data on the number of children working in Indonesian factories are hard to obtain, but it is clear that children represent a significant part of the factory workforce.

Conditions in the factories are often very poor. Safety standards are low, and accidents are common. Many workers develop respiratory problems or hearing problems as a result of working in a dusty, poorly ventilated, or noisy environment without proper protection. In some factories, closed-circuit television cameras monitor the time that workers spend in the toilet. Although by law overtime is a voluntary undertaking, in practice it is often compulsory. Several child workers interviewed in recent research said they had suffered physical or verbal abuse, and nearly one-third of the girls interviewed reported being sexually abused at work. Although many of these conditions apply equally to adult workers, unhealthy or dangerous working conditions and long hours have a more harmful impact on young people.

A fair day's pay ...

Regulations on working conditions are even more difficult to enforce in smaller workshops. Dwi Jaya Abadi is a medium-sized leather-goods business in Tanggulangin, on the outskirts of Surabaya, producing and selling high-quality bags, wallets, and shoes for the domestic and overseas markets. Behind the smart, air-conditioned showroom is the workshop, where a staff of 60 or so men and women are at work. It is extremely hot and poorly ventilated. A group of women are assembling handbags, and the air is thick with fumes from the glue they are using. They work six days a week, with no sick pay or holiday pay. Women are paid less than men for the same tasks: 'Maybe men have a greater responsibility to support their families', says the manager. 'We don't think it's fair', say the women.

► Women making handbags in a leather-goods workshop on the outskirts of Surabaya. Smaller workshops such as this are often less well regulated than the large factories, and conditions for workers can be poor.

MARSINAH

Marsinah was a 25-year-old labour-rights activist who worked at a watch factory in East Java. She disappeared on 5 May 1993, the day after taking part in negotiations to end a dispute over the company's failure to comply with an order from the provincial Governor to raise workers' wages. Her mutilated body was discovered three days later, 200 kilometres from the factory. She had been raped and tortured.

The murder investigation progressed slowly, and the authorities seemed to be trying to understate both Marsinah's role in the strike, and the possible relationship between the strike action and the murder. Many labour-rights activists and human-rights groups suspected military involvement in Marsinah's murder, and were concerned about the lack of police impartiality. Managers from the factory were eventually tried and convicted of her murder, but there were widespread claims that confessions were extracted under torture. By 1995 the government could no longer defend the convictions, and all the defendants were released. To date, no new prosecution has been instigated. Marsinah has become a hero of the labour movement, but many other women are prevented or discouraged from playing an active role in labour organisations, either because of family commitments, or because unions tend to focus on issues of importance to men, rather than women.

Trade-union activity in Indonesia was severely limited under the New Order. A code of '*Pancasila* industrial relations' emphasised harmony between workers and management, and the prevention of conflict. Only one union was officially sanctioned, and industrial action was heavily restricted. Since the early 1990s, unofficial unions have begun to fight for workers' rights, especially for fair pay and decent, safe working conditions. However, continuing military and police involvement in labour disputes often results in intimidation and violence. One NGO activist working in this field comments that '*the language of human rights means little to the authorities*'.

▼ *Surabaya's red-light district is said to be among the largest in South-East Asia. The brothels support a large community of small traders in an otherwise poor area.*

Selling sex in Surabaya

It is around 6pm in Surabaya. The setting sun casts a fiery glow across the city. Rickshaws pedal back and forth in the streets, as office and factory workers head home from work. Food stalls do a brisk trade. But one corner of the city is just waking up – the working day is about to begin. Dolly, and the slightly more downmarket Jarak, are two parallel streets, linked by a maze of small alleys. This area of Surabaya is reportedly the most extensive red-light district in South-East Asia.

ANA'S STORY

Ana is 20 years old. She arrived in Dolly from her village in East Java just two weeks ago. Brokers came to her village and asked if anyone wanted to work in Surabaya. She came here with another girl, thinking that they would be found domestic work or jobs in a beauty parlour or hairdressing salon. Instead they entered a brothel. They can earn around Rp100,000 (about £7.50) for each client. The 14 girls in her house start work around 7pm, sitting on a raised sofa in a front room with a large window, so prospective clients can see them all. They usually finish around 3am. It's really boring, she says, waiting like that, and it's hard to stay awake, but the TV is on, and loud music is blaring out. An older woman and her husband run the house, looking after the girls and cooking for them, and there are several other men in the house, who guard the girls from unpleasant clients.

The girls have an account with the brothel and can often run up big debts – indeed, debts are encouraged – so that the girls have to stay and work them off. As well as drinks and snacks, it is tempting to buy new clothes and electronic equipment. Ana hasn't yet been paid anything, but in a couple of months she will be able to go home for a visit, and she should be able to send money home. Her little room is covered in the usual posters of pop stars, and she is proud of a new hairband that she has just bought. A friend pops in with a blouse to lend her. Ana was bored in junior high school and didn't want to continue to senior high school. Her village, she says, is pretty quiet – but she's counting the days until she can visit home.

▲ *Ana and her friend relax and enjoy the early-evening scene from the roof of the brothel where they work in Surabaya.*

Liliek Sulistyowati is the director of Abdi Asih, a local NGO which works with marginalised women and children, especially sex workers. She explains that prostitution should not be seen as a special case. *'The reason why young women arrive from the villages to work in brothels is the same as the reason why they turn up in factories and workshops. They are seeking a better life for themselves and their families.'*

Nevertheless, women working in Surabaya's brothels are particularly vulnerable to exploitation and health risks. A mobile clinic visits the area every week, providing antibiotic injections and other treatment. The use of condoms is not widespread, despite Abdi Asih's health-education work, which also teaches sex workers about the dangers of over-using antibiotics and raises awareness of HIV/AIDS and other sexually transmitted diseases. Although rates of infection are not yet very high – only five confirmed cases of HIV/AIDS have so far been reported – the profits are high enough here to encourage women to continue to work after they have been infected.

The small alleyways between the main streets of Dolly and Jarak have a very mixed population. There are private houses, small shops, beauty parlours, hairdressers, food stalls, and even a mosque. There is a close relationship between the brothels and the rest of the community:

the sex workers need the services and facilities in the neighbourhood, and local traders benefit from the wealthier people whom the brothels attract into an otherwise poor neighbourhood. The area is a rich source of bribes for the city authorities, as brothel owners must make regular payments to avoid raids. There is also a local community security force, paid for by monthly contributions from the brothels. When Abdi Asih began running classes in cooking, hairdressing, and sewing, to provide women with skills for earning a living outside prostitution, it met with considerable opposition from community officials. Local inhabitants were worried that, if the sex workers left, their departure would affect the fortunes of the whole community.

▼ *These women work from home, carving wooden figures for Ibu Nyoman to sell through her showroom in Tegalalang, Bali. They are paid a daily piece-rate.*

Rural business

Outside the large cities, many small traders run family businesses, ranging from make-shift kiosks selling daily necessities to specialist businesses producing for an overseas market. Nyoman Rusi has been dealing in wooden handcrafts in the Balinese village of Tegallalang, near the tourist centre of Ubud, for the last eight years. Her shop acts mainly as a showroom and warehouse, from which she supplies bulk orders of carved animal figures and furniture to buyers from across the world. One buyer comes from the Czech Republic every three months. Her stock is produced by local craftsmen who work at home for daily piece-rates. The carvings are then finished at the shop: sanded, painted, and varnished by hand. '*Most popular at the moment are giraffes, snakes and turtles – the more traditional masks and statues seem to have gone out of fashion*', Ibu Nyoman laughs. '*But the Balinese are very clever with their hands, and will make anything for you if you come with an idea or a picture.*' The profit margin on these bulk purchases is not great, unlike the large mark-ups charged in the tourist shops in Ubud, but there is the added security of regular orders. Over her years of trading, she has seen the community grow from only four or five shops to a whole street, and competition is increasingly fierce.

Although Ibu Nyoman's goods are destined for retail abroad, she herself does not export anything directly. Her business relies on what visiting customers are willing to pay. One is a Canadian who lives in Bali and sells products overseas via the Internet. There is a danger that small traders like Ibu Nyoman will lose out to those with better access to new technology, which could connect them to a wider market. The Indonesian government recently announced plans to help farmers to gain access to global markets and pricing information through the Internet, but it admitted that this would not be feasible for smaller individual operators. The same could also be true for small traders in other sectors.

Ibu Wayan works as a labourer in a limestone quarry in Bali. Her job is to collect rocks as they are loosened by the excavators and load them on to waiting trucks. In Bali it is common to see women working as building labourers and in quarries, carrying stones balanced on their heads. It is extremely hot, there is no shade, and the nearest hospital is several miles away. The quarry is worked by a concession, and the company pays piece-rates. Ibu Wayan used to work in a Chinese restaurant, but '*I got bored, and wanted a change*'. Other workers had less choice. One man used to work in a bank in the exclusive tourist resort of Nusa Dua. He lost his job during the monetary crisis. He moved to work in a hotel, but when it eventually went bankrupt, he came to the quarry. Many people labouring in the quarry used to have office jobs, he says.

▶ *This limestone quarry in Bali, where men and women work collecting rocks for the building trade, is only a few kilometres from the exclusive tourist resort of Nusa Dua.*

Indonesia in conflict: the end of the nation?

Since 1998 the cracks in the unified veneer of the Indonesian State have begun to show in particularly ugly ways. Compounded by economic hardship and increasingly intense competition for resources, tensions which had lain dormant for decades, suppressed by the New Order regime, began to come to the surface, provoking inter-ethnic and inter-religious conflict in several areas. Anxious to protect their communities against exploitation or marginalisation, and seeing no other way to make their voices heard, increasing numbers of people have begun to identify with separatist or ethnic movements. Too often, conflict has found expression in violence.

▼ *Police on an operation in Surabaya. In some areas, a loss of faith in the official system is leading communities to organise their own 'security' forces to protect citizens and administer justice.*

Since independence, civilians have consistently been the main casualties, even the targets, of conflict. Violence against civilians has been used by the armed forces to contain and discourage separatist movements, and to maintain control over the population as a whole, while rebel groups too have used violence to intimidate local communities. Violence against women, including rape and sexual slavery, has been employed as a weapon of war, especially in East Timor and Aceh.

There has been a growing militarisation of Indonesian society, with the establishment of civil militias, ostensibly to prevent mob violence during the 1999 elections. In parts of Java and Bali, vigilante forces have begun administering rough justice to transgressors, such is the loss of faith in the police and legal system. Arming civilians has become a new medium for State violence, with the military suspected of mobilising, arming, and supporting militia groups in East Timor, Maluku, and West Papua.

In some areas, perceived threats to power and livelihoods have resulted in attempts to drive out settlers in the name of ethnic empowerment. In West Kalimantan in 1997 and 1999, and Central Kalimantan in 2001, transmigrants and spontaneous settlers from the island of Madura, who had lived in the region for many years, were the victims of violent attacks by indigenous Dayak people. Many Madurese were forced to leave the region.

Independence for West Papua?

In several regions, tension has manifested itself in demands for secession from the republic, often with some historical justification. West Papua (formerly Irian Jaya) was given to Indonesia by the UN in 1963, after the Dutch had surrendered their claim to the territory, on the condition that a plebiscite would be held within six years for the Papuan people to choose independence or union with Indonesia. Instead of allowing every citizen to vote, the Indonesian authorities appointed 1000 delegates to an electoral college; the resulting 'Act of Free Choice', held in 1969, was, according to the Indonesians, a clear vote in favour of union. Critics say the government fixed the result by bribing and intimidating the delegates. Since then, a guerrilla force, OPM (*Operasi Papua Merdeka* – Free Papua Movement) has conducted a separatist struggle, largely ignored by the outside world. As a result of the conflict, large numbers of Papuans have been killed, detained without trial, or forced to leave their homes. Those who remain face continuing insecurity and the fear of persecution.

West Papua is a poor and underdeveloped province, despite its exceptional wealth of natural resources. It is the home of Freeport Indonesia, one of the world's richest mines, exploiting enormous reserves of copper and gold. Yet indigenous Papuans have the lowest life expectancy and highest maternal mortality rates in Indonesia. They are dismissed as 'primitive' by the government; swamped by transmigrants, who now form

90 per cent of the urban population of West Papua; and controlled by non-Papuan officials. With very little opportunity to defend their interests through participation in the political process, Papuans see independence as their only chance to take control of their own future.

Aceh: the struggle goes on

The designation of Aceh as an area of military operation (*Daerah Operasi Militer* – DOM) ended in 1998, but this has not reduced levels of violence there. In fact, the separatist movement, GAM, has intensified its operations. Under President Habibie a large-scale withdrawal of troops began, and he even apologised for the brutality of the military during DOM. Anger at the excesses of DOM has, however, consolidated support for the rebels. A peaceful student-led movement calling for a referendum on independence gathered momentum for a while. The government now proposes that the province should keep 80 per cent of the locally generated revenue, but critics suspect that these concessions are a deliberate attempt to deflect calls for genuine self-determination.

The conflict in Aceh is said to have claimed around 30,000 lives since 1988. Recent attempts by international mediators to bring the two sides together for talks have had limited success. The fact that the Indonesian government is participating at all suggests that it now recognises GAM as a real political force, rather than regarding it as a mere criminal element. However, the negotiations have not reduced armed conflict on the ground, and this is a war in which most of the victims continue to be civilians. Both sides have an interest in prolonging the conflict, not only as a means of maintaining their legitimacy, but also as a way of safeguarding their income. Meanwhile, a climate of fear continues to pervade the area, as people struggle to maintain their livelihoods despite threats of violence, coercion, and deprivation. Food shortages are a constant risk in an area where it can be dangerous for farmers to tend their fields, for fear of attack or abduction. Possibly even more damaging, however, is the atmosphere of suspicion and lack of trust within communities torn apart by years of violence.

Neighbours at war: the conflict in Maluku

Violence between Christian and Muslim communities in Maluku broke out in January 1999; by mid-2002 it had claimed at least 7000 lives. Sparked by a trivial argument over a bus fare on Ambon, the violence spread to many areas in central and north Maluku. Hundreds of thousands of people have been forced to leave their homes as a result of the conflict; thousands of houses and other buildings have been destroyed, and the local economy is in ruins. Although a peace agreement was signed in February 2002, not all parties were satisfied by its terms. At the time of writing, lasting peace was still more an aspiration than a reality.

▲ *A Koran class for Muslim children in a makeshift schoolroom in Ambon city. Children throughout Maluku now study in segregated schools.*

Many people were surprised that conflict broke out here at all. With roughly equal numbers of Muslims and Christians, Maluku had been seen as a model of inter-religious harmony. However, in recent years, transmigration and spontaneous migration had tipped the demographic balance slightly in favour of the Muslims. In a region largely neglected by the private sector, the government and the official bureaucracy are the major employers and almost the sole sources of influence and access to resources. As their population grew, the Muslims became increasingly aware that they were under-represented in government and civil-service positions. A policy designed to rectify this caused resentment in the Christian community. The increasing difficulty of making a living, as a result of the economic crisis, led each side to encroach on the other's traditional areas of economic activity. Adding to the tension, both Christians and indigenous Muslims were becoming resentful of migrants, whom they accused of taking their jobs and opportunities.

As the grip of authoritarian rule from Jakarta relaxed, there was an increased opportunity to vent these frustrations physically. Access to small arms, once very difficult for civilians in Indonesia, has become much easier in recent years. The weapons used by both sides soon shifted from homemade Molotov cocktails and knives to standard-issue guns and grenades. Children have been directly involved in the fighting, employed as arsonists because they are small and fast. Since the violence began, a 'cleansing' process has resulted in religious exclusion in most areas. Children attend segregated schools and have very little chance to mix with children from the other side. Many people fear that this is storing up trouble for the future.

Outside influence

The easy availability of arms is an indication of the involvement of other parties in this conflict. Many external provocateurs have been suggested, including the military, politicians, and religious groups. In April 2000, Laskar Jihad, a militant Islamic force organised and trained in central Java, arrived in Maluku, ostensibly to provide humanitarian assistance to victims of the conflict. Laskar Jihad troops have remained in the region and are widely reported to have contributed to the continuing violence. On the Christian side, the radical separatist group FKM maintains a provocative stance.

The other principal actor in the conflict has been the armed forces. A state of civil emergency was declared in Maluku in June 2000. The vacuum of authority left by an inept provincial administration was filled by the military, which has signally failed to contain the violence. It has been suggested that certain senior military figures might have an interest in prolonging unrest in areas like Maluku, in order to safeguard the military's position in relation to the government. Certainly, individual soldiers have been charged with provoking, supporting, and even actively participating in violent incidents in Maluku.

Local peace-building

Whoever is provoking and prolonging the conflict, the population in Maluku has had enough and is looking for a way out. The new political climate in Indonesia may not have achieved much in the fight against corruption and human-rights abuses, but at least now these are topics for open debate. With the relaxation of media censorship, people are better informed than ever before about violent events in politically charged contexts.

Nevertheless, the systematic disempowerment of local-level institutions during the Suharto era has left local communities ill-equipped to contribute to peace-building initiatives. Most efforts tend to address the superficial symptoms of conflict – violence, displacement, failure of essential services – rather than the underlying causes, such as abuse of military and police power, and the lack of strong civilian leadership. In Maluku, while some local conflict-resolution activities have been successful in rural areas, many have struggled with the complexity of conflict in a crowded urban context, and have found it difficult to re-establish trust in a community racked by fear and suspicion.

▼ *Caught in a fragment of a mirror: the image of a displaced person, living with his family in a cramped room in a settlement in Ambon*

WORKING TOGETHER IN A DIVIDED CITY

Every afternoon at five o'clock in an Ambon hotel, a team of volunteers meets to discuss its work. The team was established by Baileo, an Ambonese NGO, within a week of the first outbreak of violence in January 1999, to help those affected by the conflict. It began with just seven members, both Muslims and Christians. As the conflict spread, and more and more people were displaced, the team grew; there are now around 50 volunteers.

Linda Holle, a university economics student, chairs the meeting. There is a friendly, relaxed atmosphere, but the team is serious about its work. The volunteers have been involved in many aspects of the emergency relief programme in Ambon, including health care, water and sanitation, and information and documentation. They have also contributed to a campaign to end violence against women and children, and have played a role in some of the peace-building initiatives. Today the volunteers are discussing the results of a pilot questionnaire survey to assess the psycho-social impact of the conflict on displaced populations. There is plenty of enthusiasm, but also occasional hints of the pressure of living and working in a divided city, with constant fears about security. 'We're bored with living like this', says Linda, her smile fading for a moment.

The volunteers have learned a lot about the anger and fear that rule people's lives in Maluku today. 'The most valuable lesson I have learned from the activities of the volunteer team is to be able to understand the attitude of someone who occasionally gets swept along by their emotions', says Kace, one of the volunteers. 'But for me this is a spur to continue working without reward to help people who are suffering.'

The Ambon volunteers are ordinary people, coming together at the local level to make a practical difference under difficult circumstances. At the same time, the team provides a rare opportunity for young people from the two communities to meet, exchange ideas, and work together for a brighter future.

As the military – taking its orders from central government – is effectively in charge in areas of unrest such as Maluku, Aceh, and West Papua, the notion of regional autonomy becomes practically meaningless. Ironically, those regions that most need an element of self-determination and control over their resources are precisely those that are least likely to benefit from the recent legislation.

Caught between two worlds: Indonesia's internally displaced

Between 1999 and 2001 more than one million people were forced to leave their homes as a result of conflict in Aceh, Kalimantan, Sulawesi, Maluku, and East Timor. Of these, around three-quarters – 800,000 people – have remained displaced for more than one year, with no clear prospect of either going home or being permanently resettled elsewhere. Leo Desariah is one of them. He and his family fled from Ambon soon after the violence broke out there in 1999. They arrived in Baubau, on Buton island, with only the clothes that they were wearing. This is the second time Leo has experienced terrible violence. He remembers as a small boy being saved from a bloodbath by his grandfather, during a pro-independence uprising in 1950 in South Maluku.

Although both Leo and his parents were born on Ambon, they are descended from Butonese immigrants. They see themselves as distinct from the Ambonese, and tried to stay neutral during the conflict, although migrant communities were the target of much resentment. On the other hand, they have 'returned' to Buton, along with many other ethnic Butonese, but are finding it difficult to identify with the local population: they speak Ambonese Malay, not the local language, and some don't even know which villages their ancestors came from. With no family connections, many people had no choice but to settle in government camps.

▼ Leo Desariah, leader of Wakonti camp, Buton

Leo is the leader of Wakonti camp, just outside Baubau. It has been home to 250 families for the last three years. The camp was hurriedly established by the government when the first internally displaced people (IDPs) began to arrive. It's rather crowded, but people have constructed houses for themselves, and the streets are neat and tidy. Relations with the local community are not good: permanent residents have accused the IDPs of cutting down trees from the watershed behind the camp. Leo admits that some people may have planted crops there when they first arrived – '*It was an emergency, after all*'. Now the IDPs claim that they don't even use wood for cooking, while locals cut trees to make houses. Despite these problems, no one in Wakonti has any plans to

▲ A street in Wakonti camp, Buton. Conditions for displaced people vary: in this camp, residents are fairly well-off materially, but uncertain about their future.

return to live in Ambon in the near future. '*Why would we want to?*', asks Leo. '*We don't want to be a minority group again.*' Although people do go back periodically to check on their property and family, the memories of the violence are still fresh.

An uncertain future

The alternative, however, is far from clear. When the displaced people arrived, the government agreed to allow them to use the land on which they settled for five years. Now there are only two years left, and no one knows what will happen after that. Leo explains that the IDPs are very willing to make their own efforts, as long as they have support from the government in such matters as the provision of water supplies – and electricity, so that children can do their homework at night. '*We are not poor, but not well-off either*', he says.

Leo's story is not unusual. For many IDPs in Indonesia, escaping from conflict is just the beginning of years of hardship and uncertainty. The government, insisting that providing assistance encourages IDPs to remain displaced, has introduced a policy of eradicating the problem of IDPs altogether, either through resettlement or through return. In many areas the quality of humanitarian assistance falls below international standards, and IDPs are not given the information that they need to help them to decide whether to return home or be resettled elsewhere. There are fears that resettlement of large numbers of IDPs in a revival of the transmigration programme could contribute to further tension and unrest in the future. Homeless and vulnerable, displaced people risk becoming a new marginal class within Indonesian society.

Will Indonesia fall apart?

Some people see the increase in conflict as an indication that Indonesia's days as a unitary nation-state are numbered. But rumours of its imminent disintegration have proved premature in the past. The crises of 1998 resulted in renewed enthusiasm for party politics and a high electoral turnout, rather than catastrophic violence and rupture. Even if the current unrest in certain areas does not presage a descent into generalised civil war, Indonesia can expect to experience conflict into the foreseeable future. While the triangle of mutual benefit between the bureaucracy, the private sector, and the military continues to function, there is every chance that local populations will continue to find their interests overlooked. As long as the army has an interest in proving its indispensability to the civilian administration in Jakarta, there will be no concerted effort to resolve conflict and bring offenders to justice.

The international community, including the World Bank and foreign governments, has for decades clung to a 'modernisation' model of development. It turned a blind eye to abuses of human rights in Indonesia, insisting that stability and economic growth would produce an active middle class which would defend human rights and bring about a more democratic society. As an Asian tiger economy, Indonesia was seen as a model case – not to mention a major customer of Western arms manufacturers. Despite the failure of modernisation to encourage a more liberal political climate and benefit the general population, these basic assumptions have not essentially changed. Now, the fact that Indonesia is in a 'transitional' state is seen as a reason for not challenging the government on its record of State-sponsored human-rights abuses, for fear that this may impede economic recovery.

None of this suggests that there will be much external pressure on the Indonesian authorities to control abuses of power and resolve conflict swiftly and peacefully; nor that the impetus for change is likely to arise from within. Meanwhile, Indonesians will need to come to terms with a much more fragmented idea of State and nationhood.

The future of Indonesian democracy

Reform of the political system is just the first step towards a functioning democracy. The next is to nurture a healthy civil society, where a variety of social and political organisations actively promote the interests of ordinary people and hold the government to account. The Suharto regime worked hard to dismantle social institutions and discourage non-State associations of any kind. It was virtually impossible for non-government organisations (NGOs) to criticise the government in any way. Since 1998 hundreds of new NGOs have collaborated with trade unions, women's organisations, and traditional social organisations to work towards a brighter future for all Indonesians.

Traditional social organisations

▼ A women's credit group, Sumba. A local NGO provides funding, advice, and training.

Although modern-style NGOs were heavily restricted under the New Order, many traditional methods of community support were permitted to continue. One example is *arisan*: informal savings and credit clubs operating in many Indonesian communities, where members – often women – meet regularly and make contributions to the fund, which is 'won' by each member in turn. The *arisan* is a useful way for people who find it hard to borrow from a bank to obtain small amounts of capital with which to buy school uniforms, for example, or start a small business. Many labour-intensive tasks in the village, such as harvesting, or building a new mosque or church, are completed through a principle of *gotong royong*, or 'helping each other': everyone helps in some way, contributing labour or preparing refreshments for the workers. *Gotong royong* meant that people who were left unemployed by the economic crisis could rely on their family and community to provide support and help them to get back on their feet.

EDUCATING GIRLS IN MADURA

Ibu Djum'atul Cholisah is a member of Fatayat, the young women's branch of NU, an Islamic organisation in Bangkalan, Madura, which is working to improve education in western Madura. Many parents there prefer to give their children a faith-based education, rather than sending them to government-run schools. Most education beyond elementary level is provided by *pesantren*: private Islamic boarding schools run by Muslim clerics. There are 40,000 such schools in Indonesia, educating millions of children.

Fatayat's work is especially important for girls, in an area where many marry before they are fifteen years old. Often, families cannot afford to educate all their children, and boys are nearly always given priority. As a result, many women in Madura cannot read and write Indonesian, although they may know Arabic through religious teaching. They lack confidence in themselves, and see few alternatives to early marriage and raising a family.

Fatayat staff support local *madrasah* (Islamic schools), and conduct training sessions to help local teachers to improve their skills. One such school is Yayasan Pendidikan Islam Al-Ismailyah, a *madrasah* run by *Nahdlatul Ulama* in the village of Dabung which provides mixed elementary education as well as religious instruction. There are around 200 pupils, with roughly equal numbers of girls and boys. Fees range between Rp1000 and Rp2500 a month, although the children from the poorest families pay nothing. In the afternoons, children who attend government primary schools join the *madrasah* pupils for religious instruction. The school is slowly being rebuilt with permanent materials, and Fatayat has provided a range of books for pupils to borrow and read when they like.

Although NU at the national level is perceived to be relatively conservative, here its grassroots activities are progressive and practical. Ibu Cholisah explains that one of the best ways to reach women is not through formal education, but through teaching practical life skills such as nutrition, child care, and small-business management. Fatayat recommends women to finish their education before marriage: '*Be clever before being married*'. Many Fatayat members are teachers themselves. '*It's really important to be able to provide women with role models and alternative examples*', says Ibu Cholisah. She laughs: '*Not me though, I'm just a housewife!*'

The largest non-government organisations under the New Order were religious ones. Mass Muslim organisations like the urban *Muhammadiyah* and the rural-based *Nahdlatul Ulama* (NU), which has a membership of at least 35 million, spread across Java, Sumatra, Sulawesi, and Kalimantan, were established in the early twentieth century and drew on the traditional authority of local religious leaders. Despite periods of acting as overtly political institutions, these organisations, with a wide network of local branches, devote themselves primarily to providing education and social services at the grassroots level.

An explosion of activism

Since 1998, restrictions on rights to association have been lifted. Civil society has been quick to respond to the changed political atmosphere, playing an important role in developing proposals for political and social reform. There has been an explosion in the numbers of NGOs registered in Indonesia. A whole range of people are becoming involved for the first time in organisations which aim to fight corruption, alleviate poverty, end environmental destruction, and promote human rights. '*Everyone is setting up an NGO*', says one long-term activist, smiling.

This extraordinary blossoming of civil society does have its problems. Many of the new organisations have been established specifically to attract some of the international funding now flooding the country. They do not necessarily have strong community support, or a long-term strategy for sustainable change. There is also a danger of Indonesia's non-government sector becoming heavily dependent on foreign funding, which may make it difficult for NGOs to plan for the future with confidence.

One Indonesian organisation which has worked hard to avoid over-dependence on external funders is the Centre for Environmental Education (*Pusat Pendidikan Lingkungan Hidup* – PPLH) near Surabaya, in East Java. Twelve thousand people pass through the gates of this research and education centre every year. Local schoolchildren are free to use the library, and the centre runs courses for local farmers, companies, and government officials. '*A group from a hotel in Surabaya is here at the moment, on a team-building weekend which will also encourage the participants to think about how environmental issues relate to their work*', says Suroso, the Director. Aside from running courses, the centre also provides accommodation for tourists and travellers, and runs an organic restaurant. In this way PPLH funds 80 per cent of its own educational and environmental work. '*It's not easy to remain independent,*' says Suroso, '*but we think it's very important to do so*'.

▲ *Asmara Nababan, Secretary General of Komisi Nasional Hak Asasi Manusia – the national, independent Commission for Human Rights – on a visit to Ambon*

Housewives with a difference

Suara Ibu Peduli – The Voice of Concerned Mothers – was established in Jakarta at the height of the economic crisis in February 1998, by a group of middle-class housewives protesting at the rising price of milk in the city. Before long, SIP was providing meals for the thousands of student demonstrators whose week-long occupation of the parliament building was a crucial event in the campaign to topple President Suharto. Nowadays, SIP's activities aim to support those who are struggling with the challenges of daily life. SIP provides health and education services, and hopes to improve child nutrition and support micro-credit programmes.

Like many women's organisations in Indonesia, SIP demonstrates women's desire to redefine their role in society. Javanese tradition, in particular, requires women to be obedient wives and mothers, whose main concern is the home. Women were often affected most severely by the economic crisis, a fact which has prompted women from all backgrounds to become more politically aware, and more active in working to overcome the social problems affecting them and their families.

No going back?

Political and economic events in Indonesia since 1998 have changed the country for ever. While it has not been an easy time for Indonesians, most people have survived the turmoil, and many still have high hopes for the future. Public tolerance of government abuses is far lower than at any time during the New Order, and new legislation has made a start on reforming a corrupt and authoritarian system.

▶ *Since 1998, street protests and demonstrations have become far more common, as the public becomes less tolerant of abuses of power.*

Swara Alam (the Voice of Nature) is a radio station with a difference. Based in Kendari, in South-East Sulawesi, it was set up as a way to communicate information about local environmental issues to the public. It was started in 2000 with a budget of less than Rp2 million (about £150). In the early days, the station didn't have a proper studio – just a microphone in an office, which looked out on a chicken coop. People used to say that the breakfast show was more accurately *Swara Ayam* (the Voice of Chickens) than *Swara Alam*!

Nowadays things are far more professional. Broadcasting for 15 hours a day to Kendari and the surrounding area, the station employs five journalists and has a computer-based broadcasting system, with satellite feeds from a network of news services. Swara Alam's director is Hasrul Kokoh. He explains that the programme includes plenty of popular music, mixed with the environmental and news features, to catch people's attention and keep them listening. The idea is to reach people who would not normally think about environmental issues – for example, the controversial logging operation in the hills behind Kendari, which is contributing to erosion and increased sedimentation in the bay. *Swara Alam* is always looking for new ways of communicating its message. It even held a competition to find the best new song about the environment, and the winning entry is played regularly on the network. It broadcasts interactive discussion programmes, with government officials and leading environmentalists invited to take part, and the station is increasingly experimenting with mobile-phone text messages as a cheap way for people to participate and share their opinions.

Although many of the features have an environmental focus, the station also acts as a valuable resource for gathering and broadcasting community news and strengthening local culture. Through association with a national network of like-minded stations, *Swara Alam* is also able to broadcast features of more general interest on issues such as human rights, or local autonomy.

Hasrul Kokoh takes a very practical approach. He says they chose radio as a medium for spreading awareness of environmental issues because it is more lively than print, and a cheap way to reach a large number of people. '*The great advantage of radio is that you can listen while you are doing something else. Housewives tell us they tune in while cooking or looking after the children. You can't read a newsletter at the same time as doing household chores.*'

But if Indonesia has learned one lesson from this period, it is that democracy concerns more than mere legislation. In a country where a whole generation has been denied participation in government and decision making, the transformation into a truly democratic society will take at least another generation. This fledgling democracy is now at its most fragile. The implementation of reformist policies depends on the support of the civil service, the military, and the judiciary, which is by no means guaranteed. Continuing conflict – with the greater role for the military that it entails – and the slow pace of economic recovery also threaten to undermine the political advances made so far.

Perhaps most importantly, taking control of the future must be seen as everybody's business, and everybody's responsibility, not just the preserve of the middle- and upper-class elite. After thirty years of repression, ordinary people need to draw on both traditional and modern methods of community organisation to create grassroots organisations ready to defend people's right to a secure future. Without this, change at the top will mean little, and conditions could very easily change back.

▼ *The future of Indonesia rests as much in the hands of ordinary people as it does in those of the politicians and policy makers.*

Dates and events

Approx. one million years ago Evidence of human activity in central Java.

c.425 Buddhism reaches Sumatra.

c.770 The Salendra king Vishnu begins building Borobudur.

1292 Majapahit kingdom defeats Kublai Khan's Mongol invasion.

1300 Islam begins to spread across the archipelago.

1478 Majapahit falls into chaos.

1511 The Portuguese establish a base in Malacca and begin to build forts across eastern Indonesia.

1602 Dutch East India Company founded.

1877 Netherlands Indies Government operates at a loss from this point.

1920s Nationalist movement begins to grow.

1942 Japan invades and occupies Indonesia.

1945 Japan surrenders, Allied forces land. Sukarno declares Republic of Indonesia independent.

1949 The Netherlands recognises Indonesian sovereignty. Federated States of Indonesia created.

1950 Full independence is achieved.

1965 General Suharto takes power from Sukarno after an apparent attempted coup.

1965/6 Anti-communist purges. An estimated 500,000 people lose their lives.

1969 West Papua (former Dutch colony) becomes part of Indonesia, following the outcome of the Act of Free Choice.

1975 Portugal grants East Timor independence. Indonesia invades East Timor.

1998 The economic crisis hits with full force. Food riots and widespread unrest sweep the country. Suharto resigns. B J Habibie becomes President.

1999 East Timorese vote for independence. Violence breaks out in Maluku. Indonesia holds first democratic elections since 1955: Abdurrahman Wahid becomes President.

2001 Abdurrahman Wahid impeached by Parliament. Megawati Sukarnoputri becomes President.

Facts and figures

Land area
1.9 million km²

Population
203 million (preliminary analysis of 2000 census)

Annual population growth rate
1.4 per cent (1996–2000 average)

Urban population as proportion of total
40 per cent

Under-five mortality per 1000 live births
52 (1999)

Life expectancy
Female 67.7 years; male 63.9 years (1999)

Adult literacy rate
Female 81 per cent; male 91.5 per cent

Primary-school enrolment
95 per cent (1999)

Secondary-school enrolment
55 per cent (1999)

Government expenditure on health care
0.7 per cent of GDP (1999)
16 doctors per 100,000 people

Currency
Rupiah (Rp)

Exchange rate (2000 average):
Rp8422 = US$1

Gross Domestic Product (GDP)
US$ 153 billion (2000)

GDP per capita
US$ 3040 (2000)

Annual GDP growth rate
4.8 per cent (2000)

Human Development Index ranking
110 of 173 in 2002 – calculated in terms of life expectancy, educational attainment, and real income

Major exports (2000)
Manufactures (67 per cent of total);
oil and gas products (23%);
minerals (4.9%);
unprocessed agricultural products (4.4%)

(*Sources:* UNDP Human Development Report 2002; *The Economist Intelligence Unit*)

◀ *A mural on a café wall in Bali is a reminder of the importance of tourism to the Indonesian economy*

Further reading

Books

Benedict Anderson (1990) *Language and Power: Exploring Political Cultures in Indonesia,* Ithaca: Cornell University Press

Dan La Botz (2001) *Made in Indonesia: Indonesian Workers Since Suharto,* Cambridge MA: South End Press

Robert Cribb and Colin Brown (1995) *Modern Indonesia: A History since 1945,* London: Longman

Geoff Forrester (ed.) (1999) *Post-Soeharto Indonesia: Renewal or Chaos?,* Singapore: Institute for Southeast Asian Studies

Robert Hefner (2000) *Civil Islam: Muslims and Democratization in Indonesia,* Princeton: Princeton University Press

Multatuli (Douwes Dekker) (1987 [1860]) *Max Havelaar, or The Coffee Auctions of a Dutch Trading Company,* Harmondsworth: Penguin Books

M. C. Ricklefs (2001) *A History of Modern Indonesia Since c.1200,* third edition, Basingstoke: Palgrave

Kathryn Robinson and Sharon Bessell (eds.) (2002) *Women in Indonesia: Gender, Equity, and Development,* Singapore: Institute for Southeast Asian Studies

Adam Schwartz (2000) *A Nation in Waiting: Indonesia's Search for Stability,* second edition, St Leonard's NSW: Allen and Unwin

Pramoedya Anata Toer: *This Earth of Mankind; A Child of All Nations; Footsteps; House of Glass* (The Buru Tetralogy, published between 1980 and 1988 in Indonesian, and by Penguin in English in 1996/97)

Anna Lowenhaupt Tsing (1993) *In the Realm of the Diamond Queen: Marginality in an Out-of-the-Way Place,* Princeton: Princeton University Press

Magazines and newspapers

Inside Indonesia: Quarterly magazine published in Australia. Covers a range of social, artistic, and political issues
www.insideindonesia.org

The Jakarta Post: Respected English-language daily newspaper
www.thejakartapost.com

Latitudes: Monthly English-language magazine published in Bali, with lively coverage of Indonesian culture and social issues.
http://www.latitudesmagazine.com

Tempo: Weekly news magazine, published in Indonesian and English.
www.tempointeraktif.com

Websites

Down to Earth: UK-based organisation devoted to ecological justice in Indonesia, with a useful newsletter.
http://dte.gn.apc.org/

www.indonesianheritage.com
On-line encyclopaedia of Indonesian history and culture, with brief articles written by a range of experts.

Acknowledgements

Many people have contributed time, advice, and expertise to this book, but it would not have been possible at all without the generosity and trust of the people whom we met throughout our travels. Thanks are due to all the Oxfam GB staff in Yogya, especially Yanty Lacsana and Ferny Hapsari; Oxfam GB partners in Java, Madura, Buton, Maluku, and Sumba, especially Lina at Baileo; and Catherine Robinson and Ines Smyth in Oxford. I am indebted also to Leonard Lueras, Rizal Malik, Degung Santikarma and the Latitudes team, Gerry van Klinken, and of course Sam, Anita, and Adinda. Finally, special thanks to Tantyo Bangun, whose contribution to this book extends far beyond the photographs.

Nicola Frost

◄ *A procession at one of Bali's 20,000 Hindu temples*

Oxfam in Indonesia

Four members of Oxfam International currently operate programmes in support of poor and vulnerable communities in Indonesia.

From small beginnings in 1972, **Oxfam Great Britain** developed a programme which concentrated on the promotion of organic farming; land reform; and integrated social and economic development for poor farmers, coastal communities, and indigenous people – with a strong emphasis on gender equality which has been used as a model by other development organisations operating in Indonesia. Oxfam GB began to engage in humanitarian relief work in 1998, collaborating with other international NGOs and local partners to assist refugees from East Timor, people displaced by conflict in various areas of Indonesia, and communities affected by forest fires and droughts. From its office in Yogyakarta, Oxfam GB has promoted community-based disaster-preparedness systems, while at the same time continuing its development work to help poor farmers and small producers to gain access to markets and secure their livelihoods. The programme currently concentrates on interventions in four major fields: food and income security to support sustainable livelihoods; helping to improve access to education for girls and boys from poor families; saving lives by delivering humanitarian assistance and facilitating disaster-preparedness programmes and initiatives; and helping to shape government policy in favour of poor people and disadvantaged groups. The Oxfam GB programme covers Java-Madura, Sulawesi, East Nusa Tenggara, Aceh, and Maluku. For further information, contact Oxfam-ids@oxfam.org.id

Oxfam Community Aid Abroad, based in Australia, operates a programme in Eastern Indonesia with three main themes: disaster management, indigenous people's rights and natural resources, and the promotion of health and human rights.

CAA seeks to equip communities with the necessary skills, resources, and organisations to respond to the impact of natural disasters and social conflict. It also supports the long-term economic and social rehabilitation of communities, as well as immediate relief operations during emergencies. CAA helps indigenous people's organisations to develop the capacity to assert their basic rights to be consulted on major development projects which threaten their livelihoods and culture –

schemes such as mining ventures, hydro-electric and irrigation dams, and plantation forestry, which often exclude or exploit local people.

Local campaigns are complemented by lobbying and advocacy conducted by regional and national organisations on behalf of the most threatened communities. Thirdly, CAA promotes the rights of women in situations of conflict. Working with local partners in East and West Timor in recent years, it has developed community-based systems for providing counselling and support for women who are victims of violence during times of social and political upheaval, and has advocated the rights of such women in national and international forums. It has also established community health activities, based on local women's groups, in several areas of Eastern Indonesia. For more information, contact enquire@caa.org.au

Oxfam-Hong Kong began substantive engagement in Indonesia in 2000, by funding a disaster-management programme in the east. Currently its activities focus on three inter-related themes: sustainable livelihoods, disaster management, and governance and democratisation.

It works with partners to advocate national policy change in favour of poor people; promotes popular education on democratisation and other related issues; supports participatory development planning at the local government level; and promotes community-based disaster management and conflict management/peace-building. These partners are based in Jakarta, Bandung, and West Timor. Oxfam-Hong Kong has a small project fund for the support of small-scale, one-off initiatives related to its three priority themes and specific gender-related concerns. Its Indonesia programme is managed by a programme officer based in Hong Kong. For further information, visit www.oxfam.org.hk

Novib has been funding Indonesian NGOs since the early 1960s. At the national level, its main partners are working on issues of gender, human rights, environment, debt, and political reform. These large national partners implement training and education programmes in Indonesia, but they are also involved in national and international advocacy activities. Novib funds a large NGO network in Maluku (working on emergencies, community reconciliation, and rehabilitation); and partners in Java (support for farmers and credit groups), Kalimantan (indigenous people's land rights), Aceh (credit groups and gender equality), Sumatra (labour issues), and West Papua (environment).

At home in the Netherlands, the historic links between the two countries have led Novib to build structural relations with Indonesian organisations: for example, with a Maluku organisation it is implementing education and information programmes in Holland; and it is working closely with the so-called Indonesia House in Amsterdam.

Novib's Indonesia programme is managed from the Netherlands. An integrated Indonesia Working Group in Novib co-ordinates the activities of partners in Indonesia and in Holland. For more information, contact www.novib.nl

Index